Jacob Cats, Robert Farlie

Moral Emblems

Jacob Cats, Robert Farlie

Moral Emblems

ISBN/EAN: 9783741163661

Manufactured in Europe, USA, Canada, Australia, Japa

Cover: Foto ©Thomas Meinert / pixelio.de

Manufactured and distributed by brebook publishing software
(www.brebook.com)

Jacob Cats, Robert Farlie

Moral Emblems

MORAL EMBLEMS

'TIS THE RICHES OF MIND ONLY

THAT MAKE A MAN RICH AND HAPPY.

GOOD TREE, GOOD FRUIT.

MORAL
EMBLEMS

WITH

APHORISMS, ADAGES, AND PROVERBS,
OF ALL AGES AND NATIONS,

FROM

JACOB CATS AND ROBERT FARLIE.

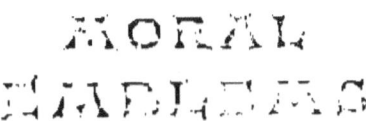

WITH ILLUSTRATIONS FREELY RENDERED,

FROM DESIGNS FOUND IN THEIR WORKS,

BY JOHN LEIGHTON, F.S.A.

THE WHOLE

TRANSLATED AND EDITED, WITH ADDITIONS,

BY RICHARD PIGOT,

Member of the Leyden Society of Netherlands Literature.

THIRD EDITION.

LONDON:

1860.

TO

WILLIAM STIRLING, ESQ^{RE}. (OF KEIR) M.P.

A LEARNED COLLECTOR OF THE PROVER-

BIAL PHILOSOPHY OF ALL AGES AND

NATIONS, THIS ATTEMPT TO REVIVE

A LOVE FOR EMBLEMATICAL

LITERATURE AND ART

IS DEDICATED

BY

JOHN LEIGHTON.

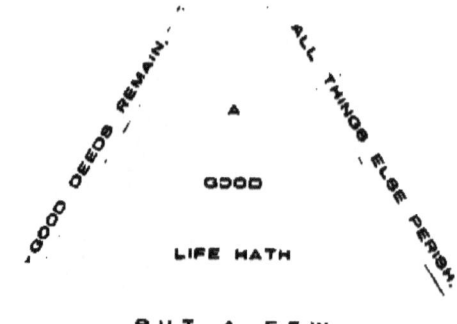

A

GOOD

LIFE HATH

BUT A FEW

DAYS, BUT A GOOD

NAME ENDURETH

FOR EVER.

Ecclus.
xli.
_13._

PREFACE TO THE SECOND EDITION.

THE reception given to the First Edition (1860) of this selection from the Emblematic Poems of Jacob Cats has already called for a reprint of the book : and the expression of a wish on the part of many readers for a more detailed account of his writings than was given in the Introduction to the First Edition, has led to the belief that a few remarks on the motives that led him to the choice of his subjects, and the method he followed in the execution of his task, may not be without interest.

The plan of the present Volume, as a selection from several works, not only precluded an adherence to the original order of the pieces selected, but tended in some degree to conceal the unity of purpose that underlies the whole series. The Emblematic Writings of Jacob Cats form no mere collection of Fables or Parables strung together at random : they are the result of wide observation and mature thought, and embody a whole system of Moral Philosophy. Few writings more completely bring before us a man who has striven to act up to a high standard of Christian duty, and whom the memory of his own struggles has impelled to warn, instruct, and encourage others. With this design, he has not merely made use of familiar facts or incidents in the physical world to enforce a lesson in morals ; he has not merely, like older writers, exposed the follies or the vices of men under fables and allegories, but he has carefully analysed the several stages in human life, and adapted his teaching to the needs and the dangers of each. But, living in an age in which the profession of a moral purpose sufficed generally to deter readers from opening a book, he felt that he must draw attention to his work by something like a stratagem. If, however, he prefixed to his "Sinne en Minne Beelden" the title of "Proteus," he did so not merely to suit the fashion of his time, but to express the general view he had taken of human life. To him that life appeared to be divided into three distinct stages, in the first of which the natural affections and sentiments predominate, while in the second, the man feels himself concerned in the wider interests of his fellow-citizens ; and in the third turns his thoughts to that unseen world which he is so soon to enter. The first stage is the season of love and marriage ; the second is taken up with the discharge of civil duties ; while the third is the period of devout meditation, in which the man is drawn away from the world into more immediate communion with God. These stages he accepts as an appointed order : the first is to him as pure and fitting as the last ; and the idea of urging on a premature development

FAMÆ MENDACIA RIDET.

Preface to the Second Edition.

of the second or the third is wholly absent from his mind. Without the slightest tinge of monastic or ascetic philosophy, he sums up for each his conclusion, that "in the natural man we should live temperately; in the civic man, justly; and in the Christian man, godly."

If the form of his "Proteus" was suggested by the prevailing taste for Emblematic writing which had already produced a literature of its own, yet the completion of his design bears evidence of his personal growth in a simple and manly piety. In his youth he had, in his own words, "penned some Amatory Emblems, that is, foolish conceits, which at the time were laid aside." These he afterwards found among some old papers, and seeing in them "the mirror of his condition in the wild season of youth," he resolved to associate with the Emblems of Love certain other Emblems more in accordance with his later dispositions, and so to depict the changeful course of human life, that men might learn, in passing from one stage to another, to replace their former inclinations by higher and better desires. And if he sought to impress on his readers a high standard of duty by fable and allegory, he felt that he was following the example of the Divine Teacher, who, under the images of seed-time and harvest, conveyed His warnings to a careless generation.

His work was done: what its success might be, he knew not; but, with a true humility, he adds, "this we know; that a firm resolve has sprung up within us to strive daily more and more towards the change and renovation of our dispositions and life in Christ Jesus." He had taught and trained himself, before he came forward to teach and instruct others; and he was content to let his work go forth in the hope that, it might impart to his readers something more than the amusement of a passing hour.

When the mind proposes honourable ends, not only the virtues, but the deities also, are ready to assist.—*Lord Bacon.*

INTRODUCTION.

ALTHOUGH the Typification of Moral truths and Doctrines by Symbolical Images and Devices had its origin in remote antiquity, and subsequently became a favourite method of imparting counsel and instruction with the Greeks and Romans, it was not until the middle of the sixteenth century that it began to assume (first in Italy) the character of a distinct kind of literature.

Towards the end of that century, the poetic genius of the erudite Andrea Alciati, of Milan, imparted so pleasing an impress to this new style of literature, as to direct thereto the attention of men of letters, with whom it soon became a favourite medium for the diffusion and popularization of moral maxims applicable to all the phases and circumstances of human life.

The Emblems of Alciati, written in Latin verse, and eulogized by such men as Erasmus, Julius Scaliger, Toscan, Neander, and Borrichius, were soon translated into the Italian, French, and German languages, and became so highly esteemed that they were publicly read in the Schools, to teach youth the Art of Emblematic writing.

Thus established, as an elegant and useful method of inculcating, both by Word and Eye-pictures, the virtues of civil life; men of learning, poets, and statesmen, in France, Holland, Germany, Spain, and England, vied with each other, as it were, throughout the seventeenth century, in the cultivation of this branch of Composition, insomuch that it had become a favourite and admired medium for the diffusion of Religious, Social, and Political maxims, and maintained that position in public favour, up to the end of the eighteenth century.

In the seventeenth century, Printing, and its sister art Engraving, had attained to Holland to a higher grade of perfection than in any other country of Europe; and, favoured by circumstances so auxiliary to the artistic illustration of works in the then not inaptly termed "Picture Language," the poetic genius of a Jacob Cats found, in the pencils of Jan and Adrian Van De Venne, and the burins of Matham, Peter de Jode, Venstralen, Van Bremden, and others, artistic exponents worthy of his muse, and equal to his most ardent desires.

Introduction.

D. Jacob Cats, the eminent Dutch Jurisconsult, Statesman, and Poet, was born at Brouwershaven in the Isle of Schouwen, province of Zeeland, on the 10th November, 1577. His father was a counsellor of some standing; and his son Jacob was first destined to the profession of the law. Having completed his course of philosophy, he proceeded to the University of Leyden, to study jurisprudence. From thence he went to France, and was some time at the University of Orleans, where he took the degree of Doctor of Laws. He subsequently went to Paris, and was very desirous to visit Italy; but his family opposed his going thither, and he was obliged to return to Holland. Arrived at the Hague, he applied himself wholly to jurisprudence, and was assiduous in his attendance at the Public Pleadings of the most distinguished lawyers. To perfect himself still more in his profession, he put himself under the direction of the juriconsult, Cornelius Van der Pol, one of the most eminent pleaders of the Dutch Bar. Some time afterwards, Cats practised with distinction at Zieuwrikzee, and at Brouwershaven. At this period it would seem he applied himself no less assiduously to Poetry, and not only became distinguished among the literati of Holland for the purity and elegance of his Latin verses, but soon took rank as one of her first lyrists in his native tongue. Falling seriously ill of an hectic fever, induced by over-application to study, he was advised by his physicians to seek a change of air.

Hereupon he repaired to England, and visited the Universities of Cambridge and Oxford. When in London he consulted the then celebrated physician, Dr. Butter, on the subject of the obstinate fever which still afflicted him; but that physician was not more fortunate in his prescriptions than those of Holland. Upon his return to his native country, he was eventually cured, says his biographer, Moreri, by an old alchemyst.

Distinguishing himself by his legislatorial and statesmanlike qualifications, no less than he had done by his poetic genius, Jacob Cats rose subsequently to high Official rank, and for several years filled the post of State Pensionary and Chief Magistrate of Middleburg and Dordrecht. He was eventually promoted to the rank of State Counsellor and Grand Pensionary of the province of West Friesland, and made Keeper of the Great Seal of Holland. After filling these important Offices for eighteen years, having now attained the age of seventy-two, he requested permission to retire into private life; which was at length granted by the States. His valuable services were, nevertheless, once more required, and he was solicited to form a member of the Embassy sent at that time to England, to arrange a treaty of commerce between the two countries. After discharging the important duties therein delegated to him, he retired wholly into private life, and devoted himself with faculties still unimpaired to the Muses, up to the advanced age of eighty-three years, when he may be said to have expired with the pen in his hand. Few men have left behind them greater proofs of indefatigable industry than Jacob Cats; and his numerous lyrical works are as rich in poetic genius as they are replete with evidence of world-knowledge, and genial with the love of mankind.

Introduction.

Would the limits allotted to this Introduction permit of a more detailed account of the life and works of this highly gifted, good man, numerous incidents and passages in both might be adduced, which would awaken in the breasts of Englishmen and women (for he was especially the poetic champion of the worth and virtues of the fair sex) an appreciation and esteem of his genius and character, as great almost as that felt for him in his own country: where "Father Cats," as he is affectionately called, is honoured as the bard of Home and of the Domestic hearth, the still popular and revered instructor of his countrymen in the Virtues of Social life, and in the Maxims of purest world-wisdom.

The "Moral Emblems" of Jacob Cats, to which Daniel Heinsius rendered his tribute of eulogy, as also two of Holland's greatest lyrists, Hoogstraaten and Zeeuwen, are almost unknown, even by name, in England, from being chiefly written in the Dutch language, of which it has been truly said, that "it has been a language too hastily neglected and despised by Englishmen."

They form, nevertheless, in the collect, a series of the most admirable compositions in Emblematic Literature which any language can boast, though written at a period when the Dutch tongue, like the rest of the northern European languages, was yet rigid and quaint in its structure, and so different in its orthographical style and idiom to the Dutch of the present day, that to most modern Dutch scholars his earlier works are almost a sealed book. Nevertheless, when Cats wrote in the vernacular of his day, the Dutch language, like that of his contemporary, Shakespeare, had been developing capabilities of harmony combined with vigour of expression, quite equal to our own, as an exponent of poetic thought and imagery, and was one in which no writer of his day knew better how to speak to the feelings of his countrymen, and win their hearts by the pleasantly conveyed wisdom of his "household words" than Jacob Cats.

By his "Sinne en Minne Beelden," and his "Emblemata Moralia et Œconomica," Jacob Cats first established his fame, both as a classical writer, an amiable moralist, and a popular poet. The former written in Dutch and Latin verse, each theme accompanied by a short distich in French verse, gave evidence both of the versatility of his poetic genius and of his linguistic talent. The success achieved by these compositions encouraged him to carry out his predilection for this style of writing in a yet more extended form; and some time after he gave to the world his "Spiegel van den Voorleden en Tegenwoordigen Tyt," or "Mirror of the Past and Present Time," in which he emblematised, in Dutch verse, the numerous proverbs and sayings of antiquity, together with the most popular and current adages of his day, in most of the European languages.

The above-named Emblematic works comprise many hundred subjects, in the treatment of which he evinced as much ingenuity as poetic grace, in working them out so as to render them a charming Code of Moral Instruction, addressed alike to the Youth of both sexes, and applicable to every phase of Civil and Political life.

INGENIO STAT SINE MORTE DECUS.

A GOOD NAME IS THE PROPER EFFECT AND REWARD OF GOODNESS.

PRAISE IS THE REFLECTED RAY OF VIRTUE.

Introduction.

To every subject of his Word-Pictures, he appends, in support of the moral he inculcates, the most pertinent quotations from the Ancient writers, and a most interesting collect of Popular adages, bearing upon the sense of each theme.

From so rich a mine of Emblematic lore, the present volume forms, of course, but a selection from each of the above-named series, the subjects of which could not therefore be placed in the same order as in the originals; but embodied in the present form will, it is hoped, be found a pleasing collect, well calculated to give an idea of the diversity of subject treated by the Author.

Sir Joshua Reynolds, when a youth, was much influenced by the Artistic excellence of Adrian Van de Venne's Designs for the illustration of the Dutch Folio Edition of Cats' Works, of which he made careful copies; and Sir Wm. Beechy, in his Life of Reynolds, states that "Sir Joshua's richest store was Jacob Cats' Book of Emblems, which his grandmother, a native of Holland, had brought with her from that country."

The Proverbs of the different nations,—that wisdom which of all others sprang from the bosom of the Peoples in every land, and was handed down from generation to generation, rather orally than by books,—form so pleasing and instructive a feature in the Emblems of Cats, that they have been for the most part preserved in their literal garb of Cats' day, an adhesion to the original which it is believed will have a greater charm and interest for the student of Languages, curious to see the shape in which the traditionally acquired wisdom of long past days was expressed, until it reached us in the more polished garb of modern times.

Whenever admissible, passages from English and other Authors, having an affinity in sense, and moral, to the Emblem or theme, have been introduced, by way of elaborating, or giving more extension to the doctrine inculcated by the Author. The appendage to this selection from Cats' Moral Emblems of a reprint of the now exceedingly rare and curious Poems and Emblems of his contemporary Emblematist, the pious Scot, ROBERT FARLIE, published in London under the title of "Lychnocausia," in 1638, will, it is hoped, be considered a not unpleasing associate for the Dutch moralist, and their juxtaposition in the same volume give an additional interest to the whole.

THE TRANSLATOR.

CULTIVATION IS AS NECESSARY TO THE MIND AS FOOD IS TO THE BODY.

THE WISE MAN REIGNS IN THE SOULS AND HEARTS OF MEN.

EMOLLIT MORES, NEC SINIT ESSE FEROS.

xii

LIST OF

CONTENTS AND ILLUSTRATIONS.

MANY MEN, MANY MINDS.

Contents and Illustrations.

ALL ARTS AND SCIENCES OWE THEIR WORTH

TO THE LOVE OF THE BEAUTIFUL.

Contents and Illustrations.

Contents and Illustrations.

NO CROSS, NO CROWN.

WER GEWINNEN WILL, LERNE VERTRAGEN.

CI E CHI VEDE MALE, E VOREBBE VEDER PEGGIO.

MORAL EMBLEMS

SPARE TO SPEAK AND SPARE TO SPEED.

TIME WILL TEACH HIM

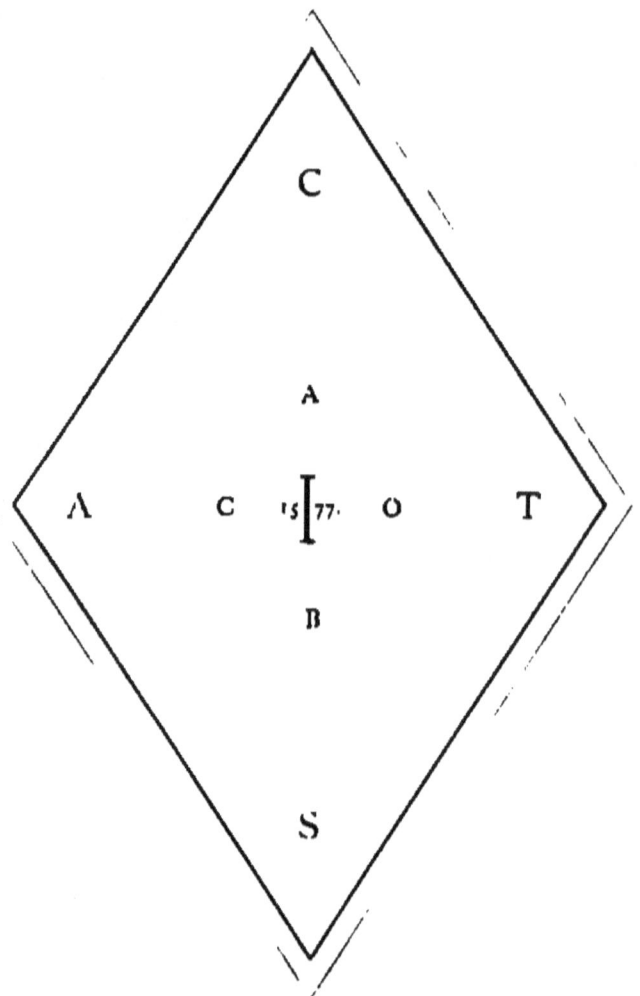

SIEHE ERST AUF DICH, DANN RICHTE MICH.

TUTTO EL CERVELLO NON E IN UNA TESTA.

C

A

A   C   ˹5 | 77˼   O   T

B

S

WHO HAS NO TEACHER.

WITH HONOUR, FAITH, AND WITH THE EYE, TRIFLE NOT.

On ne peut décrotter sa robe sans emporter le poil.

QUIEN LA FAMA HA PERDIDO, MUERTO ANDA EN LA VIDA.

HE WHO HAS LOST HIS REPUTATION IS A DEAD MAN AMONG THE LIVING.

NONE CAN CLEAN THEIR DRESS FROM STAIN,
BUT SOME BLEMISH WILL REMAIN.

HOW I've splaſh'd and ſoil'd my gown,
With this gadding through the town!
How bedraggled is my ſkirt,
Trapeſing through the hye-ſtreet's dirt:
In what a ſtate for me to be,
From this Town-life gaiety!

EHRE, GLAUBE, UND AUGE, KEIN SCHERTZ.

Come girls here, come all I know,
Playmates mine, advise me, shew
In this plight that I'm come to,
What is best for me to do?
How shall I remove this stain,
And restore my gown again?

If to wash it out I try—
Washing shrinks the cloth when dry;
Makes the colour often fade,
Or else gives a darker shade:
If I cut it out, there'll be
Such a hole that all must see:
If I rub it hard, 'twill take
All the nap off then, and make
Yet more plain, the stain that ne'er
Honest maiden's dress should bear.
Pray then tell me, some of you,
What in this mishap to do?
Thus so slut-like to be stain'd,
Makes me of myself asham'd;
For wherever I may go,
People will look at me so,—
And think perhaps,—such dirt to see,
I'm not what I ought to be.

Say, can none of you suggest,
What in such a case is best?
No?—then this I plainly see,
You must warning take by me!
If you would not soil your gown,
Go not gadding through the town:
In the streets who plays the flirt,
Never yet escaped some dirt:—
Run not therefore East and West,
Home for girls is much the best.

Maidens, wherefoe'er you go,
Walking, travelling to and fro;
Over land or over fea,
In whatever way it be;
In the Country or the Town,
Over meadow, dale or down,
Over hill or over moor,
In the houfe or out of door,
Over road or over ftreet,
Girls, where'er you bend your feet,
Keep your Clothes and Kirtles neat.

A GOOD name is rather to be chosen than great riches, and loving favour rather than silver and gold.—*Proverbs* xxii. 1.

Redire, cum periit, nescit pudor.—SENEC. *Agam.*

Ego illum periisse puto, cui perill pudor.—PLAUT.

Omnia si perdas; famam servare memento;
  Qua semel amissa postea nullus eris.
Etiam sanato vulnere cicatrix manet.

Although the wound be healed, it always leaves a scar.

Of schoon de wond'al is genesen,
Daer sal noch al een teycken wesen.—*Old Dutch Proverb.*

Die in een quaet geruchte kommt, is half gehangen.—*Ibid.*

Who comes to an evil repute is half hanged.

Give a dog a bad name and hang him.

CONDUCT thyself always with the same prudence, as though thou wert observed by ten eyes, and pointed at by ten fingers.—CONFUCIUS

PUT a curb upon thy desires if thou would'st not fall into some disorder.—ARISTOTLE.

IT is better to be poor, and not have been wanting in discretion, than to attain the summit of our wishes by a loose conduct.—DIOGENES.

BE discreet in your discourse, but much more in your actions; the first evaporates, the latter endure for ever.—PHOCYLIDES.

SHUN the society of the depraved, lest you follow their pernicious example, and lose yourself with them.—PLATO.

Feet is feet. Honour is tender.
The finest silk will spoil the soonest.

Celle n'est pas entièrement chaste qui fait douter de sa pudicité.

c

BEFORE my Light was to the winds a ſcorne,
My body likewiſe ſubject to be torne;
Now for a ſafeguard I this lanterne have,
So whilſt I ſhine from wrong it doth me ſave;
Even as the Diamond his light forth ſends,
And with his hardneſſe ſtill himſelfe defends.

 Honour is ſubject to unconſtant chance,
 Nor can it without envy 't ſelfe advance:
 Vertue to honour is a braſen wall,
 Guarded with which, it is not hurt at all;
 And how ſo ever Fortun's ſtormes doe blow,
 Yet Glory lurking thus, his light can ſhow.

FARLIE's Emblems.

FEMME 'BOTTE SE CONNAIT A LA COTTE.

A FOOLISH WOMAN IS KNOWN BY HER DRESS.

Fac Sapias, et Liber eris.

FOOLS GROW WITHOUT WATERING.

EVERY FOOL IS PLEASED WITH HIS BAUBLE.

ACT WISELY, AND THOU SHALL'T BE FREE.

MUCH men do is Folly merely;
 And if aſked the reaſon, why?
  Seldom, truthfully and clearly,
To the queſtion they reply.
If reply they make, 'tis ever,
With them all, the ſame excuſe;
And ſome think the anſwer clever:
" 'Tis the Faſhion "—" cuſtom "—" uſe ! "

Thus it ever is with fools;
Custom more than Reason rules:
And where Reason should be law,
Fashion—Customs, light as straw,
Stronger chains on them impose,
Bonds more binding far than those,
Tyrants since the world began,
Laid upon their fellow man.
He vainly boasts that he is free,
  Who fears t' infringe on Fashion's rule;
For worse than slave, already, he
  Is both at once—a slave, and fool.

INTER causas malorum nostrorum est, quòd vivimus ad exempla, nec ratione componimur, sed consuetudine abducimur. Quod pauci faciunt, nolumus imitari; quùm plures facere cœperunt, quasi honestius sit, quia frequentius, sequimur, et recti apud nos locum tenet error; &c.—SEN. *Epist.* 58.

Qui veut, il peut.

WHAT less, than Fool, and greater Fool, than he,
  Who knows no Heaven but his mistress' smiles,
And bows his reason to the tyranny
  Of her caprice and ever changing wiles!
Than he, whose brain-sick fantasy can find
  Subject for Love, in each insensate whim,
And in her very faults of heart and mind,
  A grace, to none apparent but to him!
Who sees not, when she most affects the Dove,
  She but derides the passion he reveals;
And that most false when most she vows her love,
  'Tis but to seem what least she is—and feels.
If true that, he who wills it may be free;
  Who hath no Will, must have a lack of brains;
A straw-tied Fool! who for his stultity,
  In Love, as in aught else, deserves his chains.

A wise man's heart is at his right hand, but a fool's heart is at his left.- *Ecclesiastes* x. 2.

H E that sendeth a message by the hand of a Fool, cutteth off the feet, and drinketh damage.—*Proverbs* xxvi. 6.

As a dog returneth to his vomit, so a Fool returneth to his folly.—*Proverbs* xxvi. 11.

Non ex omni ligno fit Mercurius.
Magna Negotia viris magnis committenda.

By so much the more are we inwardly foolish, by how much we strive to seem outwardly wise.—S. Greg.

Ex thymbrâ nemo lanceam conficiet;
Neque ex Socrate bonum militem.—Athen. *lib.* v.

TH' upward soaring spirit ever
　　Craves the joys of heaven to know,
But alas! the vain endeavour!
Bondslave of the flesh, below:
　　Though they be but frail as straw,
　　Worldly joys more strongly draw.

For, brethren, ye have been called unto liberty; only use not liberty for an occasion to the flesh, but by love serve one another.—*Galatians* v. 13.

The weak may be laughed out of anything but their weakness.—M. de Genlis.

WE talk of acquiring a habit! we should rather say being acquired by it. Habit is the janissary power in man! Passion and Principle the antagonist revolutionary powers for evil and for good.

YOU may as well go stand upon the beach,
　　And bid the main flood 'bate his usual height;
You may as well use question with the wolf,
Why he hath made the ewe bleat for the lamb;
You may as well forbid the mountain pines
To wag their high tops, and to make a noise
When they are fretted with the gusts of heaven,
As seek to soften that (than which what's harder?)
A foolish heart.—Shakespeare.

A Nation deserves no better laws than those it will submit to.—Goethe.

The Nation, like the man who would be free,
Must merit first the rights of liberty.

WHOSE purchafe was his pouch, his houfe a tun,
   Criticke of actions whattoever done,
That learned dogge, at noone-tyde tinn'd his light,
Searching for one, whofe actions were upright.
The Eagles young ones by the Sunne are try'd,
Mens actions by the lamp are best espy'd;
For men in day time mafkt with vizards goe,
Of truth and faith making an outward fhow.
But when they can nights fecret filence find,
Before the lamp they doe unmafke their mind.
   Happy is he whom Sunne and Lamp fees one,
   Who's honeft ftill, though witneffe there be none.

FARLIE's *Emblems.*

Domina, quo me vocat, aura.

VIENTO Y VENTURA POCO DURA.

WHITHER THE BREATH OF MY MISTRESS CALLS ME.

SPORT of thy miſtreſs' fickle mind,
   Hapleſs lover! turning ever
Like the wevell with the wind,
   Haſt not ſtrength ſuch bonds to ſever?

Look around thee, ſenſeleſs lover!—
   Fair as ſhe thou'lt many find;
Many who poſſeſs moreover,
   Far more charms of heart and mind.

OU QUE SPIRE, ME TIRE.

Slave of her defpot frown or fmile;
Haft no other will to guide thee,
Than her changeful will, who while
Ruling thee, doth but deride thee?

He who thus fubjects his reafon
To a fickle woman's rule,
Merits juft as much derifion
As the witlefs ftraw-tied fool.

QUAM miferè fervit, cui mulier imperat, cui leges imponit, præscribit, jubet, vetat quod videtur; qui nihil imperanti negare poteft, nil recufare; poscit, dandum est; ejicit, abeundum; vocat, veniendum; minatur, extimescendum?—CICERO.

Imponit leges valiibus illa tuis.—OVID.

Quo nos Numen agit.
Whither God directs us.

HE is the wifeft, who has school'd his mind
T' adopt the current of the ruling wind.
Blow whence it will, prepared for all event,
With fortune's difpenfations e'er content,
Who with difcernment both in time and place,
Bends his opinion with a cheerful grace;
To him unknown the troubles which impart
The conftant fever of the ftubborn heart,
That 'mid a world of change would ftand aloof,
To ftem the torrent with his vain reproof.
To change opinion and yet conftant be,
Is poffible alone to fuch as he
Whose ftrength of mind is in its pliancy.

UT acerbitates multas ac moleftias evitemus, confilia ad eventus ac tempora flectenda funt.—SENECA.

Oportet enim tanquàm in talorum jactu, ad id quod ceciderit, res tuas accommodare.
PLATO.

Leve fit quod bene fertur onus.—OVID.
Quoniam id fieri quod vis non poteft, velis id quod poffis.—TERENCE.
Tempori enim cedere, id eft neceffitati parere, femper fapientis habitum eft.—CICERO.
Decet id pati æquo animo;
Si id facietis, levior labos erit.—PLAUTUS.

THROW aside prejudice and thou art saved. Who prevents thee from doing so?—MARCUS AURELIUS.

ALL things change—You yourself continually change, and destroy yourself in some part. It is the same with the whole world.

WE should take counsel of reason upon that which befalls us, and correct by our prudent conduct the injustice of fortune, as a gamester repairs a stroke of ill luck by his skill.—PLATO.

A SURE means to become inaccessible to disappointment, is to become penetrated with the inconstancy of fortune, and to be prepared for all her capriciousness.—PLUTARCH.

Necessitati ne quidem Dū resistunt.—ERASMUS.

Les hommes légers et flottans,
Perdent toûjours leur avantage :
Aussi n'appartient-t'il qu'au sage,
De sçavoir bien prendre son temps.—GOMBERVILLE.

THE goal of yesterday will be the starting-point of to-morrow.—CARLYLE.

WHEN things will not suit our will, it is wise to suit our will to things.—*Arabic. Prov.*

ALL our undertakings should be bent in accordance with the circumstances of the moment.

In Domino quies.

Rest is in God.

FIX'D to no point, the wevell sways about,
  Obedient to th' uncertain wav'ring blast ;
But when the wind has ceas'd to blow in doubt,
The wevell to one point is fix'd at last.
Vain heart ! go search the world's remotest nook,
Pry into all, examine every hook,
With equal thirst and hunger still oppress'd,
In God, the Lord, thou'lt find alone true rest.

COME unto me, all ye that labour and are heavy laden, and I will give you rest.—*Matthew xi. 28.*

WHOM have I in heaven but thee? and there is none upon earth that I desire beside thee.—*Psalm lxxiii. 15.*

TAKE my yoke upon you and learn of me ; for I am meek and lowly in heart : and ye shall find rest unto your souls ; for my yoke is easy and my burden is light.—*Matthew xi. 29, 30.*

A THOUSAND evils this my life doth ſpend;
  At length fierce Boreas thereto puts an end:
My light, my heat, my flame and all is paſt;
Onely, whilſt breathe remaines, my hope doth laſt.

  This life of ours is toſt to and againe,
  Time and unconſtant Fortune workes our bane:
  Care kils us, griefe, diſeaſes doth outweare
  This life, Death dragges us to the dolefull biere.
  Fortune takes what ſhe in the morning gave;
  Or enemies robbe and ſpoile what e're we have;
  Strength, beauty, periſh, honours flye away,
  Falſe friends, when meanes are gone, they will not ſtay.
  Hope's onely conſtant in adverſity,
  Before ſhe's kild by death, ſhe will not fly.

FARLIE'S *Emblems*.

Pauper agat caute.

LITTLE BOATS SHOULD KEEP THE SHORE—

LARGER SHIPS MAY VENTURE MORE.

IF POOR, ACT CAUTIOUSLY.

LITTLE fifh! why come you fkimming
 On the furface as you do?
Deeper down you fhould be fwimming,
 That's the fitter place for you.
Here above, great fea-mews hover,
 Keen of eye, and fwift of flight;
And for fuch as you moreover,
 Have a wondrous appetite.

Here alone, the kings of ocean
　　May with safety dare the light,
But how came you by the notion
　　Thus to brave the eagle's fight?
Every kind of little creature
　　Should its proper station know;
And your fitter place by nature,
　　Is much rather—down below.
But if little Bleaks disport them,
　　Like the porpoise and the whale,
While so heedless they comport them,
　　Danger must their lives assail:
Little fishes undertaking
　　What the great alone may do,
Like all, who their part mistaking,
　　Soon or late their folly rue.

EVERY little fish expects to become a whale. He who would be every where will
be no where.—*Danish Proverb.*

THOSE who wade in unknown waters will be sure to be drowned.

AN ounce of discretion is better than a pound of wit.

WHO always does that which pleases him,
Does not always what he ought.

SEMPRE ha torto il piu debole.
A cader va chi troppo in alto sale.

ON ne doit jamais prétendre à des droits qu'on ne sçauroit soutenir.

QUIEN siempre hace lo que quiere,
No hace siempre lo que debe.—*Spanish Proverb.*

TRASPASA el rico las leyes, y es castigado el pobre.
THE rich man transgresses the law, and the poor man is punished.

HE WHO PRETENDS TO BE MORE THAN HE IS, SHALL HAVE LESS THAN HE DESERVES.

BEWARE LEST THOU TRUST THYSELF TOO MUCH.

SEEKEST thou great things for thyself? seek them not: for, behold, I will bring evil upon all flesh, saith the Lord.—*Jeremiah* xlv. 5.

As a bird that wandereth from her nest, so is a man that wandereth from his place.—*Proverbs* xxvii. 8.

A PRUDENT man foreseeth the evil, and hideth himself; but the simple pass on, and are punished.—*Proverbs* xxvii. 12.

He that exalteth his gate seeketh destruction.—*Proverbs* xvii. 19.

WHO shall go about
    To cozen Fortune and be honourable
Without the stamp of merit! Let none presume
To wear an undeserved dignity.—SHAKESPEARE.

Poor and content, is rich, and rich enough.—*Ibid.*

THRASO is Gnatho's prey.—LORD BACON.

TRUE happiness is to no place confined,
But still is found with a contented mind.

WHEN we have reached the summit of a vain ambition, we have only reached a pinnacle where we have nothing to hope, but everything to fear.—COLTON. *Lacon.*

PARVUM parva decent.—HORACE.
    FELIX est qui sorte sua contentus vivit.—HORACE.

        NE te quæsiveris extra.—*Ibid.*

CUI non conveniat sua res, ut calceus olim,
Si pede major erit subvertet, si minor uret.—*Ibid.*

        NE quid nimis.—TERENCE.

HAUD facile emergunt quorum virtutibus obstat
        Res angusta domi.—JUVENAL.

PAUPER amet cauth, timeat maledicere pauper,
    Multaque divitibus non patienda ferat.—OVID.

QUID fait ut tutas agitaret Dædalus alas,
    Icarus immensas nomine signet aquas?
Nempe, quod hic alte, demissius ille volaret,
    Nam pennas ambo non habuere suas,
Crede mihi, bene qui latuit, bene vixit, et intra
    Fortunam debet quisque manere suam.—OVID.

NULLUM Numen abest si sit Prudentia.—JUVENAL.

LIGHT is the Torches life of heavenly kind,
  Thus to a fraile and greasie masse combind,
To which the Painter beauty doth impart,
Giving it glosse and colour from his Art.
The painting's nought, light doth the Torch commend
Which first was framed onely for this end.
    It is our mind that doth our life approve,
    Shewing our race derived from above.
    Blind Fortunes goods, kins generosity,
    Youths strength, and beauties curiosity
    Make not, unlesse the spirit doe us seafon
    With that Heav'n-bred sparkle of divine reason.

                        FARLIE's *Emblems*

REST CONTENT WHERE THOU ART.

T HERE is a Fiſh, ſo Fiſhers ſay,
    Of mood ſo giddy and ſo gay;
So fond of glare and dazzling light,
That even in the darkeſt night,
'Twill crowd thereto in ſportive play,
And e'en more ready than by day
Become the wily Fiſher's prey.

WHOSO IS WELL, LET HIM KEEP SO.

19

The Fisher who thefe fish would get,
Needs neither baited hook nor net:
A blazing torch, his only lure,
Fix'd in his boat, is far more fure
Than bow-net, feine, or hook and bait,
His fkiff in little time to freight.
For while his mates propel the boat,
As up and down the ftream they float;
The fifh enchanted with the light
That makes a mimic day of night,
From far and near toward the blaze
Directing their enraptur'd gaze,
Swim up in fhoals, and fport around,
Till giddy with delight they bound
Into the fifher's bark, and there
Forfeit their life for love of glare.
Thofe who on Love or Pleafure bent,
Leave their own home and element;
And wander far to court the grace
Or win the fmile of ftranger face,
Of whom they nothing farther know,
Than their mere outward charm and fhow;
Have frequent reafon to repent
They were not with their home content;
And like the fifhes of our tale,
Their folly, when too late, bewail.
Wooers and wooed! to both of you,
Alike applies a maxim true,
Which cannot be too oft repeated :—
Who far away a-courting goes,
Where one of t'other little knows,
Or goes to cheat—or to be cheated.

QUIEN lejos va a cazar,
O va engañado
O va a' engañar.

Fallitur ignotis, aut fallit amator in oris.

Ut cephalum Venetis fallat piscator in oris,
　Præfigit parva lumina magna reti:
Mox piscis, quà teda micat, salit, inque phaselum
　Cùm ruit, in prædam navita promptus adest.
Quid tibi cum flammis, cum alat tua regna sub undis,
　Quid salis in Cymbam stulte, natare tuam est:
Ni cupiat vel fraude capi, vel fallere quemquàm,
　Errat, in ignoto littore si quis amat.

Domus amica, domus optima.

THE finger of God points to home, and says to us all, "There is the place to find
your earthly joy!"—REV. J. ABBOTT.

IF you find a young man who does not love home, whose taste is formed for other
joys, who can see no happiness in the serene enjoyment of the domestic circle, you may
depend upon it he is not to be trusted.—*Ibid.*

'MID pleasures and palaces though we may roam,
Be it ever so humble, there's no place like home;
A charm from the sky seems to hallow us there,
Which, wherever we rove, is not met with elsewhere.
　Home! Home! sweet, sweet home!
　There's no place like home!—B. CORNWALL.

È MEGLIO DOMANDAR CHE ERRARE.

BETTER TO ASK THAN GO ASTRAY.

MY Light is best maintain'd with little Oyle,
    Too much of that which feeds me, doth me spoile.
    Deluge of waters drownes the fertile ground,
Soft dropping raines makes it with graſſe abound:
Riot in cheere, the body kils and minde,
The meaneſt fare, the beſt for both we finde:
Rather in Mica than Apollo dine,
If thou wouldſt wit and health ſtill to be thine.

FARLIE's *Emblems.*

ALL IS NOT GOLD THAT GLITTERS.

GREAT SMOKE, LITTLE ROAST.

TRUST, BEWARE WHOM.

Sensim amor sensus occupat.

LOVE TAKES POSSESSION OF THE MIND
INSENSIBLY.

THOUGH fcarce at firſt apparent to the fight,
    The words which on the tender bark we write
Yet how diſtinct, 'ere long, the letters ſhew,
In fize increaſed, as with the rind they grow!
So by degrees, as on that lettered bark,
Doth Time expand to flame, Love's flighteſt ſpark:
So to the germ of Vice in early youth,
Time gives the increaſe with the body's growth;

SLOW AND SURE.

TIME IS THE HERALD OF TRUTH.

PERFECTION IS NOT REACHED AT ONCE.

And errors deem'd at firſt too ſlight to trace,
Spread to a depth no efforts can efface.
From ſmall beginnings riſe the ſierceſt ſtrife;
Nor Love, nor Vice, at once leap into life:
The breeze at firſt ſo zephyr-like and warm,
Is but too oft the prelude of the ſtorm.
That ſo it is; how many have to grieve!—
The miſchief when full-grown we can perceive;
But how it grew—we ſcarcely can believe.

AMOR neque nos statim, neque vehementer ab initio, quemadmodum ira, invadit; neque facilè ingressus, decedit, quamvis alatus: sed sensim ingreditur ac molliter, manetque diu in sensibus.—PLUTARCH.

Labitur sensim furor in medullas,
Igne furtivo populante venas,
Non habet latam data plaga frontem,
Sed vorat tectas penitùs medullas.—SENEC. *Hippol.*

———

LONG-WAITING love doth entrance find
Into the slow-believing mind.—SYDNEY GODOLPHIN.

———

THERE is no argument of more antiquity and elegancy than is the matter of Love; for it seems to be as old as the world, and to bear date from the first time that man and woman was: therefore in this, as in the finest metal, the freshest wits have in all ages shown their best workmanship.—ROBERT WILMOT.

WE are not worst at once—the course of evil
Begins so slowly, and from such slight source,
An infant's hand might stem its breach with clay;
But let the stream get deeper, and Philosophy—
Aye, and Religion too—shall strive in vain
To turn the headlong torrent.—*Old Play.*

———

Tempus omnia revelat.
TERTULLIAN.

THERE is nothing covered that shall not be revealed; and hid that shall not be known.—*Matthew* x. 26.

———

Tenera Pietatis principia.

By degrees, until Christ be formed in you.—*Galatians* iv. 19.

TILL we all come in the unity of the Faith, and of the Knowledge of the Son of
God, unto a perfect man, unto the measure of the stature of the fulness of Christ.
—*Ephesians* iv. 13.

DESPAIR not that the writing on the tree,
So indistinct at first appear to thee:
Of one day's growth was Virtue never known;
The Light of Grace spreads by degrees alone:
Until throughout Illumin'd by its ray,
The Soul of Man made perfect in each way
By Faith and Works, is fitted to partake
The Joys of Heav'n for his Redeemer's sake.

ALTHOUGH the operations of Nature are hidden, we must acknowledge the hand of
a Power which acts in secret, as we acknowledge a force which attracts heavy bodies
to the earth, or which carries light bodies upwards.—MARCUS AURELIUS.

. . . . . . *Medium Sol aureus orbem*
Occupat, et radiis ingentibus omnia lustrat.

THE pitchy darkness of the night
Is not immediate changed to Light:—
'Ere morning shows his ruddy face,
First breaks the dawn with gentle pace;
And then, the Sun, the World's bright eye,
Rises and gradual mounts the sky;
Until at last his fullest ray,
Floods sea and earth with brightest day.

BETTER is the end of a thing than the beginning thereof; and the patient in spirit
is better than the proud in spirit.—*Ecclesiastes* vii. 8.

DESERVE SUCCESS AND YOU SHALL COMMAND IT.

QUICK AND WELL DON'T AGREE.

PRESTO E BENE NON SE CONVIENE.

THIS little rift and chap workes all my woe,
  Whilſt thorow it fierce Boreas doth blow;
A crevice is a city gate to death,
Who ſtill in ambuſh ſeekes to ſtop our breath:
  A little chink dothe drowne the loaded barke,
  A ſtately houſe is burned with a ſparke:
  And one diſeaſe doth this our health annoy,
  One wound our life is able to deſtroy:
  One ſinne can Soule and Body overthrow
  Into the hell, and darkneſſe that's below.
  Doe not a danger which is meane deſpiſe,
  From meaneſt cauſes greateſt evils ariſe.

  FARLIE'S *Emblems.*

VROEG OF LAAT KOMT DE WAARHEID AAN DEN DAG.

SOONER OR LATER, THE TRUTH COMES TO LIGHT.

ERFAHRUNG IST DIE BESTE LEHRMEISTERIN.

EXPERIENCE IS THE BEST TEACHER.

THE INEXPERT ARE WOUNDED.

AS food for man, like many other fish,
  A well dreff'd Thornback is a dainty difh;
But in the cooking, lefs of art there lies,
Than how to hold it when you've caught the prize:
For he who doth not know this fifh's ways,
And grips him juft as he would take another,

CUSTOM MAKES ALL THINGS EASY.

Moſt dearly for his want of knowledge pays
With unexpected pain, too great to ſmother:
  While the more ſkill'd and cautious fiſher, he
Seizing him firſt by one gill, then the other,
  Short work of him ſoon makes, and as you ſee,
Laughs in his ſleeve to hear his neighbour's pother.

Non omnibus omnia.

All things are not good for all.

WHO think that they the faculty poſſeſs,
  All things alike to do with like succeſs;
And that alike all things may be achiev'd,
Ne'er fail'd alike to find themselves deceiv'd.
Nor ev'ry one is apt to ev'ry thing,
Nor the same talent to the purpose bring:
To take or this or that be what it may,
Each certain thing has its own certain way.
T' achieve succeſs in all we would acquire,
Needs something else beyond the mere desire.
And when obtain'd how oft 'tis but to find,
The thing desir'd, not ſuited nor design'd
Or to our talent, health, or frame of mind.
All is not good for all, though all would be
Alike poſſeſſors of ſome thing they ſee:
What joy to one imparts and is his gain,
Is both at once another's loſs and pain,
And ev'ry day doth ſome example ſhew
That one man's weal is but another's woe.

Arte citæ remoque rates veloque reguntur,
  Arte leves currus, arte regendus amor.—Ovid I. *Amand.*
  Qui ſecundos optat eventus, dimicet arte, non caſu.—Veget. *lib.* 3 *in Prof.*
    Amabit ſapiens, cupient cæteri.—Apul. *ex Afran.*

SAVOIR C'EST POUVOIR.

Without knowledge meddle not.

Dillis helleborum certo compescere puncto
Nescius quantum ! velat hoc natura medendi.

Wilt thou mix hellebore, who doth not know
How many grains should to the mixture go ?
The art of med'cine this forbids, I trow.

Felix quem faciunt aliena pericula cautum.

THAT is a twofold knowledge, which profits alike by the folly of the foolish, and
the wisdom of the wise; it is both a shield and a sword; it borrows its security
from the darkness, and its confidence from the light.—COLTON. *Lacon.*

ONE man's meat is another man's poison.
One man's fault is another man's lesson.

IT is better to learn late than to remain ignorant.—PHOCYLIDES.

WHAT is the true good ? Knowledge.
And the true evil ? Ignorance.—SENECA.

Disappointment in Marriage.

LISTEN, I pray you, to the stories of the disappointed in marriage:—collect all their
complaints; hear their mutual reproaches! upon what fatal hinge do the greatest
part of them turn?—" They were mistaken in the person."—Some disguise either of body
or mind is seen through in the first domestic scuffle:—some fair ornament—perhaps the
very one which won the heart, *the ornament of a meek and quiet spirit*—falls off; *It is
not the Rachael for whom I have served,—Why hast thou then beguiled me?*

Be open—be honest; give yourself for what you are; conceal nothing,—varnish
nothing,—and if these fair weapons will not do,—better not conquer at all, than con-
quer for a day:—when the night is passed, 'twill ever be the same story,—*And it came
to pass, behold it was Leah!*

If the heart beguiles itself in its choice, and imagination will give excellencies
which are not the portion of flesh and blood: when the dream is over, and we awake
in the morning, it matters little whether 'tis Rachael or Leah—be the object what it
will, as it must be on the earthly side, at least, of perfection, -it will fall short of the
work of fancy, whose existence is in the clouds.

In such cases of deception, let not man exclaim as Jacob does in his,—*What is
it thou hast done unto me?*—for 'tis his own doings, and he has nothing to lay his fault
on, but the heat and poetic indiscretion of his own passions.—STERNE'S *Sermons,* vol. iv.
p. 11.

SOMETIMES I was the brood of Gold'n-haird funne,
　　More pure, more chaft, than Vefta's watchfull nunne,
　　Purer than Eaflerne gemmes, than Saphirs bright,
Purer than Ophirs gold, than Rubies light,
Purer than Pactols gravell often try'd
In fire, and furnace feven times purify'd:
But fince the fates to greafe did me combine,
His filthy dregges are judged to be mine:
　　　　For why conjunction doth contagion make,
　　　　And from th' impure the pure infection take.
　　　　The foule once plung'd into the body darke,
　　　　Forgets it was a chaft and divine fparke.

Farlie's Emblems.

Dum Trahimus, Trahimur.

DO GOOD WITH WHAT THOU HAST. OR

IT WILL DO THEE NO GOOD.

WHILE WE DRAW, WE ARE DRAWN.

I SEEK to move thee to my mind:
But in so doing, this I find;—
That 'tis not I who give to thee
The fond emotion I would see;
But thine immobility,
That moves me rather, more to thee.
Strange! that the coldness of thine heart,
Should thus to mine more warmth impart;

THINE IMMOBILITY MOVES ME.

And thus, what I would draw, to fee
Draw me, who would the drawer be!
The more thou doſt my pray'r deny,
Alas! the more I burn and ſigh,
Lamenting Love's perverſity.

Adtrahens, abſtrahor.

The Puller is pulled.

LIFE'S high-raiſ'd landmark is the firm ſet rock,
    Emblem of Him who moveth all around,
Himſelf quieſcent, yet who gives the ſhock
Of Life and Motion which throughout abound.
Man, whoſe weak hand, and as it ſuits his will,
Would pull to him that rock, ſhall ſtrive in vain,
And learn therein, his Deſtiny is ſtill
Thereto but to be drawn, howe'er he ſtrain.
Sure guide to thoſe who unreluctant hale
Their bark thereon—their toil ſhall beſt avail;
And thoſe who doubt, ſhall find it ſtill prevail.

Si nunquàm Danaën habuiſſet ahenea turris,
  Non eſſet Danaé de Jove facta parens.—*Ovid, Amor. Eleg.* 19.
Sæpe ego cùm poſſem facilem exorare puellam,
  Difficilis mentem cœpit habere meam.

――――――

Quod movet, quieſcit !

That which moves, is at reſt !

GOD the Immoveable Rock, moves all.—*Pſalm* xviii,

Every good gift and every perfect gift is from above, and cometh down from the
Father of Lights, with whom is no variableneſs neither ſhadow of turning.—*James* i. 17.

O LORD, HOW MANIFOLD ARE THY WORKS!

IN WISDOM HAST THOU MADE THEM ALL.

Omne motum non in moto movetur, sed in quiescente, et id quod movet, quiescit.

HERM. *Pymand.* cap. xi.

IMMUTABLE, yet changing all
  On high, around, below;
Immoveable, yet moving all
  The way that all should go :—

Fount of all Life and Light,
  All Good, all Love, all Grace;
Encompassing with thought and sight,
  Eternity and space :—

All Peace, all sweet repose and rest,
  Yet ever moving still
Earth, Sea, and Sky, as He knows best,
  His purpose to fulfil :—

Changeless, where endless change we see,
  Unmov'd—the Mover moves
All else in changeful harmony,
  And though unmov'd—HE LOVES.

WHAT is God? The Soul of the world. What is God? All that we see, and that we do not see. The grandeur of God is infinite; alone He is all : for He wills and directs His work.—SENECA.

AN Eternal God moves this mortal world; an Incorruptible Spirit breathes life into our frail organs.—CICERO.

WE cannot understand God other than as a simple, free Being, divested of all perishable admixture : knowing all things, impressing motion upon all, and enjoying in and of Himself an eternal activity.

How do the Heavens speak to us? In what language doth it instruct us? The seasons run their course; all is reborn, all things are renewed. It is with this eloquent silence that they discourse to us the great Secret Principle by which all is moved.—CONFUCIUS.

Mon Dieu conduise moy, par la voie ordonnée,
Je suivray volontiers, de peur qu'un fort lien
Ne m'entraîne meschant, où en homme de bien
Je pourrois arriver, suivant la destinée.

The Prayer of Epictetus. LE SIEUR DU VAIR. (*Manuel d' Epict.*)

THE HEAVENS DECLARE THE GLORY OF GOD.

K

MY light from whence it came, mounts ftill on high
  Unto the fource of light that's never dry.
    Like as the Rivers to the Ocean runne,
From whence their fecret fountaines, firft begun;
Like as the ftone doth to the center fway;
So to the Spheres my light ftill makes his way.
    No joyes, delights, and greateft weights of gold,
    Nor pampering pleafure faft our foule can hold.
    The panting foule refts not, untill it fee
    His maker God, a Tri-one Deitie.

FARLIE'S *Emblems*.

Inserte, et Averies.

QUI LE VOIT D'ARRIERE S'EN MOQUE.

TRUST NOT TO APPEARANCES.

BOTH SIDES SHOULD BE SEEN.

A MASK, seen first in front, by children's eyes,
　　Strikes them with terror and with wild surprise:
　But would'st restore to calm the urchin mind,
Avert the face, and let them see behind.
With men no less, how oft doth it appear,
The worst interpreter of things is Fear!

FEAR IS A GREAT INVENTOR.

How oft the crowds of men and women grown,
Quailing like children at fome form unknown—
Or when fome found unufual ftrikes their ear,
Fly, to meet ills far worfe than thofe they fear!
And yet how frequent, would they but reftrain
The fudden terror of their fever'd brain,
And calmer wait t' examine and to fee
The how, or end of what the thing may be;
Puerile as that which fill'd the child with dread,
They'd find the fancied peril which they fled;
And fcann'd with coolnefs, learn more probably,
That what in front is terrible to fee,
Seen from behind provokes hilarity!

— — —

Timiditas est corruptio judicii.

Seneca.

THE Imagination (fays Seneca) appals us ufually more than the thing itfelf; in like manner as the mere whizzing found of a fling frightens birds, and makes them take wing, fo are we alarmed more by the noise than by the act. As the forms of bodies appear increafed in size in mifty weather, fo are all things magnified to us by Fear: in fo much that many through fear of coming into danger, fall, daily, into the moft extreme peril. Men have been known, in peril of shipwreck, to throw themfelves overboard through fear of being drowned; drowning themfelves, therefore, in order not to be drowned, and dying to avoid death. What folly fo great (fays Seneca) as to become troubled at approaching difficulties, to fpare ourfelves no anguish, but rather call an increafe of fufferings to thofe that threaten!

PERII, interii, occidi—quo curram! quo non curram!
Tene, tene—quem! quis! nescio—nihil video.

I'm loft, undone, I'm kill'd, oh whither shall I flee!
Whither shall I not flee?
Hoh! hold! whom! what! who! I know not—I do nothing fee.

THE novelty of the danger is not unfrequently its chief and only terror.

Æquam memento rebus in arduis servare mentem.

In peril, ftill preferve an unmov'd mind,
And oft no peril in the thing you'll find.

FEAR MAY KEEP A MAN OUT OF DANGER,

BUT COURAGE ONLY CAN SUPPORT HIM IN IT.

ADHIBE rationem difficultatibus, possunt et dura molliri, et angusta laxari, et gravia scitè ferentes minùs premere.—SENECA.

TERROR absentium rerum ipsâ novitate falsô augetur; consuetudo autem et ratio efficit, ut ea, etiam quæ horrenda sunt natura, terrendi vim amittant.—PLUTARCH *in Mor.*

———

Mors larvæ similis: tremor hinc, nihil indè maligni.

1 CORINTH. XV. 55.

Death, where is thy Sting!

E'EN as the mask, in front seen, only, fills
 The mind of children with a panic fear,
So Death by men is feared: yet less of ills,
Alike of both the terrors disappear
 When seen by Reason's light on every side.
And why fear Death, ere we its nature know!
'Tis but a livid mask, which, seen behind,
Hath terrors none, but balm for every woe,
Hope, peace, and comfort to the righteous mind;
 Opening to realms more bright, the portals wide.

———

PUERI larvas timent, ignem non timent; sic nos timemus mortem quæ est larva, contemptu digna, peccatum non timemus.—CHRYSOSTOM, *Hom. 5 ad Pop.*

YEA, though I walk through the valley of the shadow of Death, I will fear no evil: for thou art with me; thy rod and thy staff comfort me.—*Psalm* xxiii. 4.

THE Lord is my light and my salvation; whom shall I fear! The Lord is the strength of my life; of whom shall I be afraid!—*Ibid.* xxvii. 1.

WHY are ye fearful, O ye of little faith!—*Matthew* viii. 26.

SIC nos in Luce timemus.—LUCRET. *l.* 2.

PRECIOUS in the sight of the Lord is the death of his saints.—*Psalm* cxvi. 15.

FOR I am in a strait betwixt two, having a desire to depart, and to be with Christ: which is far better.—*Philippians* i. 23.

NO glory could I fhew, wer't not the night
   In fable clouds did mantle up heavens light,
When ftarres are vail'd, and Phœb' her hornes doth hide,
Laying her creffet and attire afide.
The more nights fogge doth mafke the fpangled fpheare,
The more in darkeneffe doth my Light appeare;
Nights foggy cold doth make my flame more ftrong,
And light's more glorious pitchy clouds among.

    If you together contraries parallel,
    By contrary oppofition they excell.
    Vertue compare with Vice; and you fhall fee,
    This fhew his glory, that his infamie.

                FARLIE'S *Emblems.*

EXPERIENCE IS THE INSTRUCTOR OF FOOLS.

HE IS A GREAT FOOL WHO FORGETS HIMSELF.

Sibi nequam, cui bonus.

WHO IS HURTFUL TO HIMSELF,
BENEFITS NO ONE.

M AKE Love with cheerful heart,
     Of what use thoughts of sadness?
  Do as the Partridge doth,*
That fattens on Love's gladness:

* La perdrix s'engraisse à courir la femelle. PLUTARCH

HELP THYSELF, AND GOD WILL HELP THEE.

10

HE WHO SERVES THE PEOPLE HAS A BAD MASTER.

WHO SERVES THE PUBLIC SERVES NO ONE.

Do as doth the pretty bird *
Which on the banks of Nile,
The while he feafts his fill, no lefs
Doth fervice to the Crocodile.

Nay ne'er repine, fweet youth,
'Tis fenfelefs, downright Folly,
To let thine ardent flame
Give caufe for Melancholy:
He that loves and ferves a maid
In truth, achieves two ends;
For while her wifh he pleafes moft,
So he no lefs himfelf befriends.

Er puer es, nec te, quidquàm nisi ludere oportet.
Lude, decent annos mollia regna tuos.
Cur aliquis rigido fodiat sua pectora ferro?
Invidiam cædis paris amator habes.

Ovid, lib. 1. de Remed. Amor. ad Cupidinem.

Amor immoderatus ipsi amori novissimè inutiles sic facit: nam quàm frucndi cupiditate insatiabili quis flagrat, tempora suspicionibus, lachrimis, querelis perdit, otium sui facit et novissimè tibi est odio.—HIERON.

Les violences qu'on se fait pour s'empêcher d'aimer sont souvent plus cruelles que les rigueurs de ce qu'on aime.—LA ROCHEFOUCAULD.

Non id agis, quod agis.

Publica prætexuntur, privata curantur.

QUELQUE personage que l'homme Joue, il Joue toujours le sien parmy.—MICH. DE MONTAIGNE.

WITH Public men, great fault the Public find,
    That while the business of the State they do,
They shew themselves the while somewhat inclin'd
To look to self, and mend their own state too.
In this withal, we see not much to blame;
And those who most the impulse oft condemn,

— — · ·

* On the subject of this bird, the Trochilus of Pliny, see Plin. lib. 8, cap. 25. De Trochilo sive avium rege, crocodilo dentes sculpente et se saginante.

Would—ten to one—in office do the same,
  Or even worse than those whom they contemn.
In this as in all else 'tis the excess
  That constitutes the fault, and those alone
Who steer the middle course, the best express:
  "Serve well the Public ends, but serve thine own."
The wisest Statesman of a surety,
  Is he who lab'ring for the Public weal,
His own alike with the same glance can see,
  And feel for that for which none else would feel.
On this world's stage, whate'er the Part man plays,
  In act and speech however seeming fair;
He always something of his own betrays,
  And in the Part—the Man himself is there.

———

A la cour du Roy, chacun pour soy.
Sois serviteur, sans serviteur.
Onder Vrientschaps schyn, besorght hy't syn.

———

O prodiga rerum luxuries !

WHEN gorged with food, the greedy Crocodile
  Extended lies upon the sands of Nile;
The pretty King bird with an appetite
Gross as the Vulture, or the bird of Night;
Hies to the monster's wide extended jaws
To cleanse his fetid teeth with beak and claws.
That bird so pretty should a taste display
For food so filthy, doth too well pourtray
And symbolise the grosser appetites
Which some men shew for sensual delights;
And who while doing service as they seem,
The service of their bellies most esteem.

———

Whose end is destruction, whose God is their belly; and whose glory is in their shame, who mind earthly things.—*Philip.* iii. 19.

Stolen waters are sweet, and bread eaten in secret is pleasant.—*Prov.* ix. 17.

WHILST ſtormy winds about the Lanterne rage,
　　The light ought to have lurked in his cage;
Untimely love undoes him, while he lends
His Light, loe how his harmeleſſe life he ſpends.
　When troops of enemies beſiege the wall,
　For feare of hurt, ſhut gates, though friends doe call.
　It that a friend accompanyed with a foe
　Doth come, feare neighbour danger, let him goe.
　If thou lov'ſt to be charitable, doe
　So good to others, that it hurt not you.

FARLIE's Emblems.

BELF IS THE MAN.

IT'S A BAD GAME WHERE NOBODY WINS.

QUIEN QUIERE TOMAR CONVIENELE DAR.

De Kanne gaat soo lang te water, totse eens breeckt.

THE POT GOETH SO LONG TO THE WATER, TIL AT
LAST IT COMMETH BROKEN HOME.

ALAS! Alas! What have I done?
　　Oh! Woe is me this day:
My Pitcher's broke!—all from this fun,—
　　This silly, romping play.
Oh! sad! what will my Mother say?
　　Her words have come too true!

DONNA CHE PRENDE, TOSTO SE RENDE.

Left margin: REPUTATION IS GAINED BY MANY ACTS.

Right margin: BUT IS LOST BY ONE.

WHEN THE DOOR IS OPENED FOR A LITTLE VICE,

On me alone the blame she'll lay,
  Whatever shall I do?
And yet full many a time and oft,
  In this same Pitcher too,
I've water drawn both hard and soft,
  Nor had mishap to rue:
Pumpt water in and thrown it out,
  And pumpt it full again,
Nor e'en so much as chipp'd the spout,
  For Mother to complain.
Alas! that I could ever be
  So heedless of her say—
The warning she would give to me,
  And, almost ev'ry day!
But here about young fellows are
  So rollicking and free;
Pull girls about so much, nor care;
  And most of all p'rhaps me.
That Hans there of our Village, he's
  So rough and wild alway;
If I wont speak, he'll sulk, or tease
  Whene'er I pass his way.
And I'm good natur'd too I know,
  And where is then the blame,
I love a laugh sometimes, and who
  At heart but does the same?
And I and other girls when we
  Perchance together meet,
Some lads are always sure to be
  At games about the street:
And so it was just now, although
  I did all I could do,
For Water first my way to go,
  When Hans he joined us too.
Then there began a game all round
  Of running—jibe and joke,
When down we came upon the ground,
  And I my pitcher broke!

IDLE MEN TEMPT THE DEVIL.

And thus I've found the faying true,
I've many times heard spoken,
"The Pot that goes too oft unto
The Well, at laft gets broken."

TANT va la cruche à l'eau, que le manche y demeure.

Den Krug gienge so lang zur bach
Bis er zu lest zerbrach.

Der Krug gehet so lang zum brunnen, bis das er bricht.

Tanto va la secchia al pozzo, che vi lascia il manico.

Consuetur peccando sæpius pudor.

Tanto va la capra al cavolo, che vi lascia la pelle.

Hat geytjen loopt soo dickwils to de koolen, tot het eens de vacht laet.

De mag die om de keerse weeft,
't Is wonder soo die lange leeft.

Wie veel wil mallen,
Moet eenmael vallen.

Κακοῖς ὁμιλῶν αὐτὸς ἐκβήσῃ κακός.

Id est,

Malos frequentans ipse et evades malus.

Une folie en tou faite.

Lit! vrysters! wie ontrent u gaen
Een malle greep is haest gedaen.

Be cautious, maidens, how ye run;
A foolish thing is speedy done.

Avoid too much Familiarity.

IT is unwise both to use and to permit too great Familiarity. Who become familiar, soon lose the superiority which their previous reserve gave to them; and consequently, their credit. We should be familiar with none—never with our superiors, because it is dangerous; nor with our inferiors, because it is derogatory; and still less with the vulgar, whose ignorance renders them insolent, and, unable to perceive the honour that is done them, they presume that it is their due. Familiarity is one of the tendencies of a weak mind.—GRACIAN.

The purest treasure mortal times afford
Is—spotless reputation; that away,
Men are but gilded loam, or painted clay.—SHAKESPEARE, *Rich. III.*

AND loth'ſt thou me, my Soule, loving to goe
　　Elſewhere, I pray thee whither, let me know?
Was thou not all this while my deereſt mate,
My gueſt, my convoy, conſort in eſtate;
While I did floriſh, thou didſt conſtant prove,
My times are darkened now, ſo is thy love?

SOULE.　Here as a captive to a keeper, ſo
I tyed was with thee, at liſt, to goe,
Baniſht from home: loe now my bonds are looſe,
Thou dy'ſt, I glad runne to my father's houſe.

　　Soules bond with body hardly maketh breach,
　　Yet this doth dye, and that Heav'ns dwelling reach.

Farlie's Emblems.

KEEP BAD MEN'S COMPANY,

AND YOU WILL BE OF THE NUMBER.

Ludite, sed Caste.

PLAY, BUT CHASTELY.

THE cunning Hedgehog, with inſtinctive art,
   In ball-like ſhape, rolled up, upon the ground,
With open hole-like mouth, knows well his part,
T'entrap the giddy mice that ſport around.
And lo! when one, more prying than the reſt,
Draws near, to peep within a hole ſo nice,

RIRE SANS MAL-ENGIN.

The Hedgehog fnaps him up with eager zeft,
And moufey pays for peeping, in a trice!
Let caution guide your fport, be what it may;
For where expected leaft, fome fnare may lay:
And Venus' boy was painted blind of yore,
For that in darkneſs he worked miſchief more.

Formosas intueri jucundiſsimum, tangere autem et tractare sine periculo non licet.
PLUTARCH.

Amor latebricolarum hominum corruptor.—PLAUT. Tris.

Detur aliquid ætati, sit adolescentia liberior, non omnia voluptatibus denegentur.
Dummodo illa in hoc genere præscriptioque moderatioque teneatur, parcat juventus
pudicitiæ suæ, ne spoliet alienam, ne probrom castis, labem integris, infamiam bonis
inferat.—Cic. pro Mar. Cœlio.

Parva Patitur ut Magnis Potiatur.

Niuno piu facilmente inganna gli altri, che chi è solito, e ha fama, di non gli
ingannare.—GUICCIARDINI.

No one so easily deceives others as he who is expert in deceit, and has a repute
for Integrity.

He is not the greateſt cheat who begins with cheating.

TO gain his ends, the Hedgehog firft permits
    Each fportive freedom that the mouse would take:
For well he knows if he to that submits,
    More sure is he, his prey of him to make.
So is't with thoſe who moſt to wrong intend;
    They firft assume the semblance of a friend;—
And e'en sometimes to make the cheat more sure,
    Some favour offer, or some loss endure:
Till having gain'd the vantage ground they sought,
    And lull'd suspicion with moſt fair pretence,
Their too reliant dupe at length is caught,
    And rues too late his ill plac'd confidence.

Vigor ingentibus negotiis par, eb acrior, quo somnum et inertiam magis oatentat.
TACITUS.

PELLICULAM veterem retines, et fronte politus,
Abstruso rapidam gestas sub pectore vulpem.—PERS. *Satyr*. 5.

FRAUS in parvis fidem sibi præstruit, ut, cum opcræ pretium est, cum mercede
magnā fallat.—LIVY.

Objecta movent.

BE sober, be vigilant ; because your adversary the devil, as a roaring lion, walketh
about, seeking whom he may devour.—1 *Peter* v. 8.

THE Hedgehog knows the mouse's wanton ways,
   And knowing this, knos's well to profit by it :
He shows the mouse a hole, nor aught betrays
That might abate his innate bent to try it :
Within his mouth in hole-like fashion hollow'd
The mouse soon creeps—and is as quickly swallow'd.
With just such baits as these, Man's mortal foe
Lure's man to ill, and fills this world with woe :
He knows our hearts, he knows our love of sin,
And by that knowledge strives our souls to win,
Tempts each alike, by that which most allures
The heart of each, and thus his prey secures.

BUT I fear, lest by any means, as the serpent beguiled Eve through his subtilty, so
your minds should be corrupted from the simplicity that is in Christ.—2 *Corinth*. xi. 3.

IT is the Devil's part to suggest : Ours, not to consent. As oft as we resist him,
so often we overcome him : As often as we overcome him, so often we bring joy to
the Angels, and glory to God, who opposeth us, that we may contend, and assisteth
us, that we may conquer.—S. BERNARD *in Ser*.

FOURE Elements in this my body are
All yockt in one, yet ever still at warre;
As all agree to nourish this my light,
So to my ruine they combine their might:
Aire maketh way for flame, Earth builds a pyre,
My moisture feeds the still confuming fire.
Still as I shine by light, by light I dy,
As cause of life, so of mortality,
It was Prometheus fault who stole away
Heav'ns fire, and joyn'd it to his mortall clay.

    Moisture doth heat, and heat doth moisture quale,
    That dryes our body, this makes it dampe and fraile,
    That which doth give, doth likewife spend our breath;
    The first of being, is first houre of death.

                    FARLIE's *Emblems.*

UNDER THE BACKCLOTH THERE IS SOMETHING ELSE.

UPON A SLIGHT PRETEXT THE WOLF TAKES THE SHEEP.

UNDER FAIR WORDS, BEWARE OF A FRAUD.

ONE SWALLOW DOES NOT MAKE A SUMMER.

Yl, met Wyl.

HATEZ VOUS LENTEMENT.

EILE MIT WEILE.

HASTEN AT LEISURE.

THE Peach-tree with too eager haste
 To shew its blossoms to the sun,
Gives oft its pretty bloom to waste,
 Before the frosts of Spring are done.

Much wiser is the Mulberry,
 Which only thinks its leaves to shew,

UNA HIRUNDO NON FACIT VER.

When leaves are green on ev'ry tree,
And roses have begun to blow.

They most ensure Success and Praise,
Who, guided by the Rule of Reason,
Do fitting things on fitting days,
And dress as most becomes the season.

PLUTOST meurier,
Qu'amandrier.

D'Amandel bloeyt vroeg, de Moerbesy laet:
Maer let eens wie het beter gaet!

Sat cito, si sat bene.
Assez tost, si bien.

Hasat genoeg,
Ist wel genoeg.

Soon enough begun,
That which is well done.

Dress drains our Cellar dry,
And keeps our Larder lean.—Cowper.

Fond pride of Dress is sure a very curse.
Ere fancy you consult, consult your purse.—Benjamin Franklin.

The most violent Passions will sometimes allow us a respite, but Vanity leaves us
no repose.—La Rochefoucauld.

PROIN quidquid est, da tempus ac spatium tibi:
Quid ratio nequit sæpè sanavit mora.—Seneca, Agam.

Si quid benè factum velis, tempori trade.—Ibid.

Da spatium tenuemque moram, male cuncta ministrat
Impetus.—Statius.

Differ, habent parvæ commoda magna moræ.—Ovid.

The mean, is the point nearest to Wisdom: it is better not to reach it at all,
than to over-run it.—Chinese Proverb.

Let Reason guide you at all times, even in the most unimportant things.
Pythagoras.

AVOID doing that which may draw down upon you the reproaches and the envy of your neighbours.—PYTHAGORAS.

KNOW your opportunity, and do not speak before-hand of that which you will do. Should your project fail, you will furnish subject for ridicule to those who are jealous of you.—THALES.

Esto Castu modicus.

WE are told by Jewellers that there is no Diamond of so fine a water, but it requires some aid to improve its lustre. This observation has been also applied to young women.

No objection can be made thereto, provided it be understood in a fitting and healthy sense. For it is indisputable that Virtue and Modesty are the greatest ornaments or auxiliaries to the Beauty of Woman.

La chasteté est la première beauté.

EXTERNAL Show and costliness of Dress are pernicious in their effects upon the female mind, and tend to sap the principles of Virtue and Modesty. As regards her attire, the motto of a virtuous young Woman should be :—

Nitide, non delicate.

Reyn gekleet,
En niet te breet.

Clean in Dress,
Without Excess.

Ne sois Paon à toy parer,
Ny Perroquet en ton parler,
Ny Cirogne en ton manger,
Ny Oye aussi en ton marcher.

Suspecta semper ornamenta ementibus.

Veel vlaggen, luttel lesters.

WHOSE adorning let it not be that outward adorning of plaiting the hair, and of wearing of gold, or of putting on of apparel.—1 Peter iii. 3.

THE Crafts-man did me of pure tallow frame,
   And made me fit to nourish heav'ns flame;
One thing remain'd, that I should take with fire,
When season due, and fit houre doth require:
Loe how the rats catching me all alone,
With envious teeth my body ceaſe upon;
I dye before my day, they life prevent;
Before I live, my liveleſſe body's ſpent:
I dying could with teares my death bemoane,
But this untimely death doth yeeld me none.

   The infant ſo oft doth it ſelfe entombe,
   Before it ſee the day, in mothers wombe.
   So by untimely death youths hopes decayes,
   Which might have well deſerved many daies.

                              FARLIE's *Emblems.*

Luceat Lux Vestre coram Hominibus.

LET YOUR LIGHT SHINE BEFORE MEN.

ANXIOUS, tempeſt toſſ'd and weary,
　To the ſeaman's gladden'd ſight,
'Mid the night-ſtorm, what ſo cheery
As the gleaming beacon's light?

Though the wild waves wilder threaten,
Calmer now, he ſteers his way

To the long defir'd haven,
Guided by its friendly ray.

Like unto that beacon, truly,
He of upright heart and mind,
Holding high his light fhould fhew the
Heav'nward way to all mankind.

Chriftian! lift your light on high then,
Let it fhine o'er all, and fhew,
In this darkfome world to all men,
How and where that men fhould go.

LET your Light fo fhine that men feeing your good works may glorify your Father which is in Heaven.—*Matthew* v. 16.

We labour in the boifterous fea: Thou standeft upon the shore and feeft our dangers: give us grace to hold a middle course betwixt Scylla and Charybdis, that both dangers efcaped, we may arrive at our Port fecure.—S. AUGUST. *Soliloq.* cap. 35.

O LIGHT inacceffible, in respect of which my Light is utter darkness; fo reflect upon my weakness, that all the world may behold thy strength: O Majesty incomprehensible, in respect of which my glory is mere shame; fo shine upon my misery that all the world may behold thy glory.—HUGO, *Pia Defid.*

MY God, my light is dark enough at lightest,
Increase its flame, and give it strength to shine:
'Tis frail at best: 'Tis dim enough at brightest,
But 'tis its glory to be foil'd by thine.
Let others lurk: my light shall be
Propos'd to all men; and by them to Thee.

QUARLES, *Hieroglyph* viii.

H EAVEN doth with us, as we with torches do,
   Not light them for ourselves; For if our virtues
Did not go forth of us, 'twere all alike
As if we had them not. Spirits are not finely touched,
But to fine issues; nor Nature never lends
The smallest scruple of her excellence;
But, like a thrifty goddess, she determines
Herself the glory of a creditor,
Both thanks and use.—SHAKESPEARE.

So far the little candle throws its beams,
So far shines a good deed in a naughty world!

Q UI in occulto benè vivit, sed alieno profectui minimè proficit, carbo est. Qui verò
   in imitatione sanctitatis positus, lumen rectitudinis ex sese multis demonstrat,
lampas est : quia sibi ardet, et aliis lucet.—GREG. *Super Ezech.* homil. 5.

Numquam est mutila opera civis bonis.—SENECA.

Utile etiam exemplum quiescentis.

MELIUS homines exemplis docentur, quæ in primis hoc in se boni habent, quod
approbant, quæ præcipiunt, fieri posse.—PLINIUS, *Paneg.*

Doctus sine opere est ut nubes sine pluvia.—*Adag. Arab.*

Sic luceat lux vestra coram hominibus; id verò ex hoc fit, cùm apparet miseri-
cordia in affectu, benignitas in vultu, humilitas in habitu, modestia in cohabitatione,
patientia in tribulatione.—HUGO, *De Claustro Animæ,* lib. 3.

Sic agitur censura, et sic exempla parantur,
Cum judex, alios quod manet, ipse facit.— OVID.

O LORD ; who art the Light, the Way, the Truth, the Life ; in whom there is no
darkness, error, vanity, nor Death : the Light, without which there is darkness ; the
Way, without which there is wandering ; the Truth, without which there is error ; the
Life, without which there is Death : say, Lord, let there be Light, and I shall see Light,
and eschew darkness ; I shall see the Way, and avoid wandering ; I shall see the Truth,
and shun error ; I shall see Life, and escape Death : Illuminate, O illuminate my blind
Soul, which sitteth in darkness, and the shadow of Death ; and direct my feet in the way
of Peace.—S. AUGUST. *Soliloq.* cap. 4

WHEN ftormie Boreas puts the feas in rage,
    And fwelling waves inteſting warre do wage;
When fun is darken'd, when night doth heav'n confound,
And foaming billowes give a difcord found:
My light then leads the way through reeling ſtrands,
Guiding by Scyllas rocks, Charybdis fands.

    Here we are toſſed in a maine of feares;
    But Chriſt our admirall the lanterne beares;
    Leaſt we ſhould fuffer ſhipwracke in the night,
    He leads us through all dangers by his light.
    Who then woukiſt come to Heav'ns long wiſht-for bay,
    Follow thy Saviour, who's Truth, Light, and Way.

                                FARLIE's *Emblems.*

Fumo pascuntur amantes.

SMOKE IS THE FOOD OF LOVERS.

WHEN Cupid open'd Shop, the Trade he chofe
 Was juft the very one you might fuppofe.
Love keep a fhop?—his trade, Oh! quickly name!
A Dealer in tobacco—Fie for fhame!
No lefs than true, and fet afide all joke,
From oldeft time he ever dealt in Smoke;

AMANT, TON BONHEUR N'EST QUE VAPEUR.

xn

Than Smoke, no other thing he fold, or made;
Smoke all the fubſtance of his flock in trade;
His Capital all Smoke, Smoke all his ſtore,
'Twas nothing elſe; but Lovers aſk no more—
And thouſands enter daily at his door!
Hence it was ever, and it e'er will be
The trade moſt ſuited to his faculty:—
Fed by the vapours of their heart's deſire,
No other food his Votaries require;
For, that they ſeek—the Favour of the Fair,
Is unſubſtantial as the Smoke and air.

AMORES et deliciæ maturè, et celeriter deflorescunt.—CICERO *pro M. Cæl.*

Omnia speramus, promissaque vana fovemus
    Molliter: et faciles ad nova vota sumus.
Intereà totum paupertas possidet ævum,
    Cæcaque volvendo somnia, vita perit.—DANIEL HEINS.

. . . —

Love.

    — Tнɛ cheriſh'd Fire,
Which blindly creeps through every vein and dries
The fluent blood, whence groſſer vapours riſe;
Sadding the soul with fearful phantaſies.

It is to be all made of fantasy,
All made of Paſſion, and all made of wiſhes;
All adoration, beauty, and obſervance;
All humbleneſs, all patience, and impatience;
All purity, all trial, all obedience.— SHAKESPEARE.

    Love reigns a very tyrant in my heart,
    Attended on his throne by all his guards
    Of furious wiſhes, fears and nice suspicions.—OTWAY.

O MIGHTY Love! from thy unbounded power,
How ſhall the human boſom reſt ſecure?
How ſhall our thoughts avoid the various ſnares?
Or Wiſdom to our cautioned soul declare
The different ſhapes thou pleaſeſt to employ,
When bent to hurt, and certain to deſtroy!—SOLOMON.

THERE's nothing half so ſweet in Life as Love's young Dream.—MOORE.

SO DOES BEAUTY LOVE.

NEMO SOLUS, AUT DEUS, AUT DÆMON.

Love and Hope.

I HAVE heard many say :
Love lives on Hope ; they knew not what they said.
Hope is Love's Happiness, but not its Life.
How many hearts have nourished a vain flame —
In silence and in secret, though they knew
They fed the scorching fire that would consume them.—L. E. L.

> LIGHTER than air, Hope's summer visions die :
> If but a fleeting cloud obscure the sky,
> If but a beam of sober reason play ;
> Lo ! fancy's fairy frost-work melts away.—ROGERS.

SIR KENELM DIGBY, in his *Private Memoirs*, makes a lover say, " I will go to the other world to preach to damned souls that their pains are but imaginary ones, in respect of them that live in the hell of love."—P. 38.

LOVE is a species of Melancholy.—BURTON.

Cure for Love.

MRS. CARTER was for half an hour one evening entirely in love with a Dutchman ; and the next morning she took a dose of algebra fasting, which she says entirely cured her.—*Memoirs*, vol. 1. pp. 36-7.

Love and Legislation.

STRANGE, and passing strange, that the relation between the two Sexes, the Passion of Love, in short, should not be taken into deeper consideration by our Teachers and our Legislators.

People educate and legislate as if there was no such thing in the World : but ask the Priest, ask the Physician—let them reveal the amount of Moral and Physical results from this one cause.

Must Love be always discussed in blank verse, as if it were a thing to be played in Tragedies or sung in Songs—a subject for pretty Poems and wicked Novels, and had nothing to do with the prosaic current of our every day existence, our Moral Welfare and Eternal Salvation ? Must Love be ever treated with profaneness, as a mere illusion ! or with coarseness, as a mere impulse ! or with fear, as a mere disease ! or with shame, as a mere weakness ! or with levity, as a mere accident ! Whereas it is a great Mystery, and a great Necessity, lying at the foundation of Human Existence, Morality, and Happiness—mysterious, universal, inevitable as Death. Why, then, should Love be treated less seriously than Death ! It is as serious a thing.—MRS. JAMESON.

SO DOES AN IDLE PERSON LOVE.

WHO fearſt outragious Vulcans damned ire,
    And wouldſt be ſafe from night-ſurpriſing fire;
Put out the flame, the ſmoking ſnuffe ſuppreſſe,
Leaſt from the ſmoake the fire it ſelfe redreſſe;
For fire is next to ſmoake, and oft its ſcene,
That reaking ſnuffe a blazing fire hath beene.

    Who feares the damned fire of inward luſt,
    And Cupids flames, obſerve this rule he muſt.
    Hearts concupiſcence, 'fore it's vehement,
    Looke that in words he ſuffer't not to vent;
    For words are ſmoake of burning hearts deſire;
    Smother his words, he needs not feare the fire:
    But otherwayes a wanton complement,
    Doth blow his fire, and makes him give conſent.

                    FARLIE'S *Emblems.*

Sua quemque Fortuna pænitet.

EACH DEPLORES HIS OWN LOT.

THE Fish that in the Weel are taken,
    When they find no iſſue more,
Feel the ſtronger wiſh awaken
    To be where they were before:
But the Fiſh that ſee them in it,
    Think it far more pleaſant there;
And they ſtrive their beſt to win it,
    Swimming round it ev'rywhere.

THOU SHALT NOT COVET.

63

Thus it is that men, like Fifhes,
Ne'er contented with their lot,
Ever reftlefs in their wifhes,
Craving more than what they've got;—
In their greed of wealth and ftation,
Coveting yet more and more,
Oft in change of fituation,
Find it worfe than 'twas before.

PISCIS cùm modo ingrediendi naſſam videat, egrediendi non videat, et nihilominùs
ingrediatur, piſcatoribus fit præda; non eſt ergò ſuscipiendum negotium, niſi
priùs perſpectâ ratione quâ te poſsis inde rursus explicare: nec enim labyrinthi
ingrediendi ſunt ſine filo, quo securus poſsis redire.

NEMO eſt, quin ubivis, quàm ibi, ubi eſt. eſſe malit: nam suam quiſque conditionem
miſerrimam putat; cùm tamen contentum suis rebus eſſe, maximæ ſunt certiſsimæque
divitiæ.—CICERO.

Non eſſe cupidum, pecunia eſt.

Si vis gaudere per unum diem, radas barbam, ſi per ſeptimanam, vade ad nuptias;
ſi per menſem, eme pulchrum equum; ſi per ſemeſtre, eme pulchram domum; ſi per
annum, ducas pulchram uxorem; ſi per biennium, fias sacerdos; ſi ſemper vis eſſe
lætus et gaudens, vivas tua ſorte contentus.—Theaurus ridendi.

AMONG good things I prove and find
The quiet lyfe doth most abounde,
And sure to the contented mynde
There is no riches may be founde.—Songs and Sonnets.

Let not what I cannot have
My cheer of mind destroy.—COLLEY CIBBER.

ALL men have their trials and afflictions, but a contented mind accommodates itself
to every viciſsitude of life; neither poverty nor distress, neither losses nor
disappointments, neither sicknes nor sorrow, can affect its equanimity.—DR. BREWER.

A CONTENTED mind is free from the distreſsing passions of ambition, covetousness,
jealousy, envy and the like, which prey like Vultures upon the peace of the
discontented.—Ibid.

MAN always desire more than they possess, yet scarcity has been the ruin of fewer People than abundance and repletion.—THEOGNIS.

I AM richer than you, if I do not want things, which you cannot do without.
SOCRATES.

THERE is a jewel which no Indian mine can buy,
No chemic art can counterfeit;
It makes men rich in greatest poverty,
Makes water wine, turns wooden cups to gold,
The homely whistle, to sweet music's strain;
Seldom it comes, to few from heaven sent,
That much in little—all in nought—Content.
WILBYE's *Madrigals.*

If there be any happiness to be found upon earth, it is in that which we call Contentation: this is a flower that grows not in every garden: the great Doctor of the Gentiles tells us that he had it; I have learned (saith he) in what estate soever I am, therewith to be content.—BP. HALL. *Of Contentation.*

If solid happiness we prize,
Within our breast the jewel lies;
And they are fools who roam:
The world has nothing to bestow;
From our own selves our joys must flow,
And that dear place our home.
COTTON.

VAIN is alike the joy we seek,
And vain what we possess,
Unless harmonious reason tunes
The Passions into peace.

To temper'd wishes, just desires,
Is happiness confin'd;
And, deaf to folly's call, attends
The music of the mind.
CARTER.

ALL living things with others loffe maintaine
  Their life, not fo my harmleffe light I gaine.
The plant doth feede upon the fertile foile;
And brutifh beafts the pleafant plants doe fpoile;
So harmleffe beaft, and bird, and fifh muft dy,
To pamper mans too licorifh gluttony.
But of condition though I mortall be;
Yet this my Light is onely nurft by me.

   The moft of men doe live by others loffe,
   Whilft others goods they to themfelves engroffe:
   So man proves wolfe to man, and robbery gives
   Moft gaine to him, who moft unjuftly lives.
   Thrice happy's he, who's of his ftate content,
   As if it were Carffus or Crœfus rent.

                              FARLIE's *Emblems*.

A CONTENTED MIND IS A CONTINUAL FEAST.

SUCH THINGS AS YE HAVE.

Ogni Fiore al fin perde l'odore.

BEAUTY WITHOUT VIRTUE IS LIKE A ROSE WITHOUT SCENT.

ROSES AND MAIDENS SOON LOSE THEIR BLOOM

EVERY FLOWER LOSES ITS PERFUME AT LAST.

MAIDEN! will you never learn
    All the leſſons Flowers teach,
And that each of them in turn
    Hath its potent power of ſpeech?
    In the early violet's bloom,
    Modeſt mien, and ſweet perfume,

BEAUTY IS THE SUBJECT OF A BLEMISH.

In the daiſy of the mead,
If you have the mind to read,
Simple though to you they ſeem,
Each affords its moral theme!

Ev'ry Roſe that here you ſee,
 Ev'ry Flower that blooms a-field,
Whatſoe'er their Beauty be,
 Muſt alike that Beauty yield!
  Aye! believe me, maiden ſair,
  Whatſoe'er the Gard'ner's care,
  Whatſoe'er his ſkill may be,
  It but little needs, to ſee
  That which is ſo ſair to-day
  Vaniſh like a dream away!

Let there come a chilling rain,
 Nipping wind, or ſlighteſt froſt,
Few would lift their heads again—
 All their beauty would be loſt!
  Or, e'en let the Sun, whoſe light
  Calls to life their colours bright,
  But too fiercely on them ſhine,
  Straight you'll ſee their bloom decline,
  Wither'd by too great exceſs
  Of that very Sun's careſs!

Maidens! and Young Women all!
 Learn then as you ſhould from this,
All the ills that youth befall,
 And how fleeting Beauty is!
  Lips that with the coral vie,
  Witching Beauty of the eye,
  Ev'ry charm of form and face,
  Whatſoe'er their winning grace,
  Have their Emblem of decay
  In the Roſe of yeſterday!

BEAUTY MAY HAVE FAIR LEAVES, YET BITTER FRUIT.

Maiden, there is something too,
Womans Beauty ne'er defied,
Though as rich in charms as you,
  And as full of youthful pride.
    You have but to look at me,
    And you may that something see,
    That can steal away each grace,
    And in little time deface,
    Whatsoever be your care,—
    All that makes you now so fair.

Time! it is, whose stealthy wing
  Throws on all alike its shade,—
Fades the bloom of ev'ry thing,
  Howsoever fair 'twas made!
    Time! though it so softly treads,
    Silent ruin round us spreads;
    And as Age has done by me,
    If you live, you'll surely see—
    Beauty's but an idle boast,
    Your's to-day; to-morrow lost!

But, there *is* a Beauty yet,
  Far more lasting in the wear;
That which Virtue doth beget,
  Fadeless—bright—beyond compare:
    Make that Beauty your's, fair maid;
    Time o'er that can cast no shade;
    And when wrinkled that fair brow,
    'Twill be fairer far than now,—
    With a Beauty that shall gain
    Lasting Love in God's domain.

————

As for Man, his days are as grass; as a flower of the field, so he flourisheth.
  For the wind passeth over it, and it is gone; and the place thereof shall know it no
more. *Psalm* ciii. 15, 16.

PRETTINESS DIES QUICKLY.

*S*UCH is lights love to Heaven, that still above
    It mounts, and cannot to the center move;
Hold you it under, it will upward reach,
And through its ruinous body make a breach.
    Our foule doth bend our bodies ftraight and even,
    As with it felfe, it would them raife to Heaven;
    But all in vaine it undergoes fuch toyle,
    The body will not leave its native fuyle :
    Age puls it downe, and makes it floupe full low,
    Till death doth give his fatall overthrow.
    Then through the bodies breach the Soule doth rife,
    And like a conquerour, mount to the fkyes.

                    FARLIE's *Emblems.*

A WOMAN THAT PAINTS PUTS UP A BILL TO LET.

YOELE HOOP, WAKENDE DROOM.

IDLE HOPE IS A WAKING DREAM.

MANY A SLIP 'TWIXT THE CUP AND THE LIP.

SWIFT, through the flood, cheer'd by his master's praise,
    With vig'rous stroke the Spaniel cleaves his way,
    And lo! already with his ardent gaze,
He marks the wounded wild-fowl as his prey.
Near and more near upon the bird he gains,
    And as the space that parts them smaller grows,
With speed increased, he plies the foot and strains
    Towards the game, now close before his nose.

CHACUN NE PREND CE QU'IL POURCHASSE.

Then bounding high at once from out the wave
With fudden rush to feize the certain prize:
That which he thought no means of flight could fave,
Dives 'neath the flood, before his wond'ring eyes.

In Love affairs, as in intrigues at court,
It oft occurs as in the field of fport;
Almoft before the chafe we have begun,
We deem the Fair, the place, and game are won;
And when moft fure we've grafp'd the prize aright,
We fee it quickly vanifh from our fight.
'Tis not alone in fleep that dreams arife;
Our hopes are oft but dreams with waking eyes;—
As vifionlefs and vain by day as night,
We think them real, and they fade from fight,
Leaving the heart to grieve and to complain,
To find itfelf fo cheated by the brain.

———

GUERRA, caça e amores
Per um prazer cem dores.

—POTUENDI tempore in imo,
Fluctuat incertis erroribus ardor amantium.—LUCRET. lib. 4.

FALLITUR augurio spes bona sæpè suo.—OVID.

MULTA cadunt inter calicem supremaque labra.
Inter os atque escam multa interveniunt.
Inter os atque offam multa interciдunt.

NON esse sapientis præfidere constanter iis, quæ aliter evenire nata sunt.—POLYB.

FERE libenter homines id quod volunt, credunt.—CÆSAR.

O FALLACEM hominum spem, fragilemque Fortunam! et inanes nostras contentiones
quæ in medio spatio sæpè franguntur et corruunt; et antè in ipso portu obruuntur,
quàm portum contingere potuerunt.—CICERO 3. de Orat.

SPEM PRETIO NON EMAM.

Plerumque hominum proprium est quod ratione difficilè cognoscunt, id sibi cupiditate et spe facilè fingere.—Franc. Guicciard. *Hist.* lib. 4.

We readily believe what we wish. Our wishes are fathers to our thoughts. We believe unwillingly that which we do not wish.

Fortune is fond of change; she allows herself to be possessed, and she escapes from us. Dost thou suffer from her fickleness? Learn to bear it with patience.—Pythagoras.

God's Providence, alike in the Smiles and Frowns of Fortune.

Ferendum et Sperandum.

THAT Fortune is so changeful in her moods,
   Is scarcely to be blam'd in such degree
As we are wont to hear.
Did we but put the question to ourselves;
We, who do change each moment of our lives!—
In her so fickle nature we should see
That which our changeful nature best befits.
The only diff'rence lies therein; that we
Find Fortune's changes more abrupt and loud
Than those which daily in ourselves take place:
Which like the Shadow of the Dial, mark
Their silent progress—but a progress still,
Not the less certain that it seem to us
Less evident, because insensible!
Yet, mutative in body as in mind,
With faculties that change with ev'ry day
Their pow'r t' enjoy, or estimate aright
The lights and shades which fall across our path;
We still repine ungrateful for the Light,
And deem the Shadows more than we can bear:
And this withal, forgetful of that Power
Who in His Wisdom, wiser far than we,
Knew best what our frail nature would befit,
To make us that He will'd that we should be.

With humble joy bear Fortune's transient smile,
Nor let her frown to discontent beguile:
With stedfast Hope, Columbus-like, at last
Thou'lt find the New World when the storm is pass'd.

FINCHE VI E FIATO VI E SPERANZA.

73

U

WHEN as my Light with beames did brightly ſhine,
   And ſtarre-light was but equall unto mine;
I was in great requeſt and ſet above,
Was deare to all, who ſaw me, did me love:
Now breathing ſighes, and languiſhing I grone:
I'm hatefull to my ſelfe, belov'd of none.
If once againe my light beginne to burne,
With it my light and honour ſhall returne.

    When Fortune ſtanding on her ſlippery ball,
    Doth favour, then are we admir'd of all;
    But if ſhe frowne, then flatterers flye away,
    No friends abide, if once your meanes decay:
    O but if Fortune change, and ſmile againe,
    Then fawne theſe flatterers, and beare up your traine.
    Much like the Sea theſe Clients floate and flow;
    And Fortune turnes her coat, at every ſhow.

                  FARLIE's *Emblems.*

ENTRE LA BOUCHE ET LA CUILLIERE.

VIENT SOUVENT GRAND DESTOURBIER.

Amor, ut Pila, vices exigit.

LOVE, LIKE A BALL, REQUIRES TO BE
THROWN BACK.

MAIDEN fair! if you would learn
   Well to play this pleasant game;
You must strike in quick return,
   So that I may do the same.
Should you fail to strike at all,
   And that I make play alone,
Then the shuttle's sure to fall,
   And the game at once is done.

SWEET IS THE LOVE THAT MEETS RETURN.

Mark, sweet maiden, when I strike,
  And attend to what I say:
Tennis and Love's game alike
  Need a quick return of play:
Who their pleasure most would know,
  And in equal share partake,
In both games alike must shew
  Equal zest to give and take.
Love and Tennis both, play'd ill,
  Soon upon the players pall,
When *one* shews a want of will
  To hit back the flying ball.
Love, to Love is demonstrative;
  Love, gives life and strength to Love,
And in being thus creative,
  Love doth most its power prove.
Love of Love's at once the Price,
  And Reward that Love loves best;
Nothing can to Love suffice,
  But the Love that gives it rest.
If from me to Love you'd learn,
  Love; and be my Sweetheart true;
But if you give no return,
  Then I'll say—good-bye to you.

———

JAMAIS l'Amour ne se paye que par Amour réciproque.
  Et Pretium, et Merces solus Amoris Amor.

Beneficium non est aurum, sed Amor per quem datur.
Amor enim Beneficii anima.—*Vid.* Seneca *de Benef.*

Divinissimus est, quem redamare piget prius amantem.
                 August. *de Amore divino.*

LOVE WILL CREEP WHERE IT CANNOT GO.

(left margin, vertical:) LIEB OHNE GEGENLIEB IST WIE EINE FRAGE OHNE ANTWORT.

Ama à chi t'ama,
Rispond à chi ti chiama.

Antwoord dieje vraegt,
Min dieje Liefde draegt.

Answer him who calls unto you,
And love him who brings Love to you.

Una mano lava l'altra, e le due lavano il viso.

L'une main lave l'autre, et les deux le visage.

Als d'eene hand d'ander wast, soo wordense beyde reyn.

D'eene Min breng: d'ander in.

Manus manum fricat, gratia gratiam parit.

Ferro ferrum acuitur.
Fructus Amoris Amor.

Amour su cœur me poind,
Quand bien aimé je suis;
Mais aimer je ne puis,
Quand on ne m'aime point.
Chacun soit adverti
De faire comme moi;
Car d'aimer sans party,
C'est un trop grand ennoy.—Marot.

Excute mihi ignem, et allucebo tibi.—*Proverbium Arabicum ex Erpenio.*

Id est, ut Jos' Scaliger interpretatur,
Esto mihi, ero tibi.   Be mine, I will be thine.

Ut ameris, amabilis esto.—Ovid.

Aimer sans Amour est amer.
Vriendschap van eener zijde en duert niet lang.
Friendship all on one side lasts not long.

Κόλφ χεῖρα νίστει
Χάριν χάριν φέρει.

————Amare recuso,
Illum quem fieri vix puto posse meum.—Ovid. *Ep. Helen.*

Amour est d'Amour récompense,
Et celui est trop à blâmer,
Qui pour le moins (s'il ne commence)
Ne veut pas, quand on l'aime, aimer.

WHEN I this wisht-for light to tinne desire,
    I prostrate crave it from this flaming fire;
From whence if light come not in fitting time,
I am consum'd before the light be mine.
  Whose meanes are small, whom Fortune favours not,
  They take their patrons mercy for their lot;
  To them their supplications they direct,
  Attending still with homage and respect;
  Delay undo'th them, makes them spend their oyle,
  Their hopes grow lesse, and greater is their toyle;
  Unlesse their Patrons timely shew their love:
  For gifts, by timely giving, double prove.

                FARLIE'S *Emblems.*

LOVE LEVELS ALL INEQUALITIES.

LOVE GROWS WITH OBSTACLES.

FLEE LOVE, AND IT WILL FOLLOW THEE.

LOOK BEFORE YOU LEAP.

Qui Captat, Capitur.

PIU PRONTO AD ACQUISITARE, QUE PRUDENTE AD CONSIDERARE.

CHASSE PENIBLE OU LE VENEUR EST PRIS.

THE BITER BITTEN.

HIGH up in air, the ſea-mew ſpies
  An oyſter lying on the ſtrand,
Gaping with open shell t' inhale
  The ſummer breeze from off the land.
To ſeize the luſcious morſel quick-
With ſudden ſwoop and deadly pick,
The ſea-bird darts his horny beak
  Between the oyſter's ſhell:

HOLD-FAST IS A GOOD DOG.

But closing on it quick as thought,
The bird is by the oyster caught!
  And nipped so tight and well;
That strive and struggle as he may,
To free his beak, and get away;
He keeps him captive, firmly bound,
Till with return of tide he's drowned.
Who to themselves would all appropriate
Of that they see, deserve the sea-mew's fate;
Nor doth he fail to meet it, soon or late,
Whose nose is thrust in everybody's plate.

The Event is often different from the Intent.

DEFEATING our intent and expectation,
  In strange reverse of that we think to see;
When certain most,—we find ourselves mistaken,
  And he is caught, who would the catcher be.

To curb the pride and malice of man's nature,
  'Twas wise ordained, that he should sometimes see,—
In his own toils the hunter captive taken;
  And he despoiled, who would the spoiler be;—

The evil doer, 'gainst his calculation,
  By his own mischief foiled and hurt, alone,
The slander of a neighbour's reputation,
  Recoil with deeper wound upon his own.

The same in another sense.

A'eaxl run druwren, gard rwo'l rengerm.
How to retain, is more than how to gain.

THE mew is in a fix, as we have seen;
  With beak well jamm'd the oyster's shells between:
But what avails the shell-fish his success?
Strange case it is—yet nothing less than true,
His very fortune causes him distress,
Nor knows he with his capture what to do!
A very load to him, a trouble quite,
The catcher would be well-rid of the caught,
'Tis almost 'gainst his grain to hold him tight—
Yet, to let go—were perhaps with peril fraught!
Just so in life, whom management doth fail,
Success nor riches to their good avail.

HARM seek, harm find.
As you sow, so you must reap.
As you make your bed, so you must lie on it.

Qui mal cherche, mal trouve.
Ut sementem feceris, ita metes.—CICERO.
Comme on fait son lit on se couche.

Tute hoc intraisti, tibi omne est exedendum.—TERENCE.

THE Power and the Riches acquired by a life of anxious toil, slip not unfrequently from their possessor's hands, from defective government, or mismanagement: because it is easier to acquire power and to gain wealth than to keep and use them prudently when gotten. An especial virtue is needful to this, more than is required for the gradual heaping up of riches.

Non labore, sed munificentiâ Domini.
Not by labour, but by the blessing of the Lord.

THE oyster without change of place, or toil,
  Prospers in peace, and easy takes his spoil:
The sea-mew, restless, sweeps the shore and main
In quest of food, and, little oft to gain:
The oyster toils but little, yet he thrives;
The sea-mew, less from his great toil derives;
And so all labour is in vain, unless
God of his blessing doth our labour bless.

Ecclesiastes ix. 11.

I SAW under the sun, that the race is not to the swift, nor the battle to the strong, neither yet bread to the wise, nor yet riches to men of understanding, nor yet favour to men of skill; but time and chance happeneth to them all.

THE Righteousness of the upright shall deliver them; but transgressors shall be taken in their own naughtiness.—*Proverbs* xi. 6.
Go not forth hastily to strive, lest thou know not what to do in the end thereof, when thy neighbour hath put thee to shame.—*Proverbs.* xxv. 8.
WITHOUT counsel, purposes are disappointed.—*Proverbs.* xv. 22.
He that is greedy of gain, troubleth his own house.—*Proverbs.* xv. 27.

UN FOL OU BETE, FAIT BIEN CONQUETE, MAIS BON MENAGE C'EST FAIT DU SAGE.

A FOOL MAY MEET WITH GOOD FORTUNE, BUT THE WISE ONLY PROFITS BY IT.

THE glaffie gulfe joyn'd with Earth's globe in one
  Gives waters to the rivers, loofeth none;
The Sunne that makes fo many glorious dayes,
Doth loofe no light, and ſtill he waſt's his rayes:
The Loadſtone to the iron gives vertue rare,
And yet no wayes his owne he doth impaire;
So this my torch can give to others light,
And ſtill, as is his wont, ſhine perfect bright.

Thus Divine Wiſdome doth communicate
Herſelfe, that others may participate.
The good more common, better is, and grace
Wiſheth, all were partakers of her cafe.

FARLIE's *Emblems*.

Rami correcti rectificantur; trabs minimè.

CE QUE POULAIN PREND EN JEUNESSE

IL LE CONTINUE EN VIEILLESSE.

THE BRANCHES MAY BE TRAINED, BUT NOT
THE TRUNK.

AS I want wood to build a houſe,
   I would cut down this tree:
    'Tis a fine ſtem, although in truth
It ſomewhat crooked be.
I've ſunk this pole, in hopes to bend
   It ſomewhat ſtraighter by;

Yet fear, though I the trunk e'en with
A hundred withies tie—
(It is so stiff in heart and growth,)
That it will never take
A better shape, whatever be
The efforts I may make.
But while here on the ladder, I
Some person hear below!—
Some voice unknown that calls to me,
Holloa! up there! holloa!
And somehow (why I know not) I
Leave off to hear what he
Has got to say, and this is the
Discourse he holds to me:
Eh! man, what art about? wouldst bend
A full grown tree like this!
Dost take it for a sapling, eh?—
Why what's with thee amiss!
There is no sense in what thou do'st,
So spare thy labour, friend;
'Tis only when the tree is young
That thou the stem canst bend!
Go, get thee home, and rather let
Thy children have thy care:
The labour that thou here bestow'st,
Were better given there.
Those are the trees whose growth once set
Will give thee most concern;
And from th' experience of my years,
This lesson thou may'st learn:
In tender youth alone, the mind
To Virtue can be trained;
But that once pass'd, its growth and bend
Are not to be reclaim'd.

THE above adage is taken from the collection of Arabic sayings collected and translated by the learned Polyglot D. Erpenius, who was Professor in the high school of Leyden. This saying admonishes all parents and guardians that the years of childhood only are fitted for instruction, and that therefore a special regard should be had to them for that purpose. "Bend the neck of thy child whilst he is yet young, so that he become not stiff-necked," saith the Lord. Many sayings of our time, either in word or spirit, and frequently in both, correspond with that divine admonition. In allusion hereto, Scaliger in his day, cited in his Collection of Proverbs as coincident in meaning the French adage:

Vieil arbre mal aisé à redresser.

Alte Bäume sind böse zu biegen.
Alte Hunden bös bandig zu machen.
Old dogs are hard to train.

'T moet vroeg krommen dat een goede reep worden sal.
To make a good rope it must be bent early.

Men mag zijn oude schoenen verwerpen; maer niet zijn oude seden.
A man can throw away his old shoes, but not his old habits.

Gewoonte maeckt eelt.
Custom makes things hard.

Wat heeft geleert de jonger man,
Dat hangt hem al zijn leven an.
What the young has learnt sticks to him through life.

Nutritura passa natura.

Dalla matina si cognosce il buon giorno.

L'haver cura de putti
Non è mestiere de tutti.

Taurvet adeth galet mischthiuldun.—Turkish Proverb.

Id est,
It is difficult to change customs.

Γέρωττα δ' ἀρθοῦν, φλαῦρον, ὃς νέος πέσοι.
Aristoph. apud Suidam.

Id est,
Erigere durum est, qui cadit juvenis, senem.
Annosam arborem transplantare. Eodem sensu adagium refertur ab Erasmo.

Castigar vieja, y espulgar pellon, dos rivancos, son.

'Tis Education forms the common mind;
Just as the twig is bent, the tree's inclin'd.

Train up a child in the way he should go: and when he is old, he will not depart from it.—Prov. xxii. 6.

THOU goeſt about miſchiefe and ſtill doſt feare,
   Leaſt this my light 'gainſt thee ſhould witneſſe beare;
So having put me out thou think'ſt to worke
Thy will, and yet in ſecret ſtill to lurke.
   Thou art deceiv'd, the darkneſſe of this cell
   Containes a light, that ſees the loweſt hell.
   But thou a Want, canſt not perceive this light,
   Neither diſcerne Sun-ſhine from cloudy night.
   Then ſhalt thou ſee it, when the Deity
   Shall kindle that ſparke which in thy breaſt doth ly.
   What e're thou doſt, looke to that Light which made
   All Lights, and ſhines as day in midnight ſhade.

                        FARLIE's *Emblems.*

Als morsige lieden Kays werden, soo schuerense de Panne van achteren.

WHEN SLOVENLY SERVANTS GET TIDY, THEY POLISH
THE BOTTOMS OF THE SAUCEPANS.

LOOK at thefe Girls! When they firſt came to me,
   They were ſo fluttiſh and untidy both,
I never had a ſaucepan fit to fee,
   And ſcarcely ever a clean kitchen cloth.
But now it is a pleaſure to behold;
   They are become ſo wondrous clean and neat;

I never have to rate them, nor to scold,
   Nor ever now an order to repeat.
They're scouring, scrubbing things continually,
   'Tis rare indeed such girls as them to meet;
Their kitchen's quite a palace, as you see,
   And look, their dresser! isn't it a treat?
They never now require to be told
   A single thing: and, what is even more,
I'm often now almost obliged to scold,
   They've got so over nice, 'tis quite a bore!
They're now what I call cleanly to excess,
   And make themselves more work than need be made;
So much, that oft I'd rather see a mess,
   That I might have some reason to upbraid.
There, look! 'tis quite ridiculous to see
   Those pans and kettles which they're scrubbing so;
Although I've said it don't require to be,
   They clean the very bottoms of them too!
'Tis just the way with foolish people all,
   When once their old bad habits they forsake,
In th' opposite extreme too oft they fall,
   And of a virtue then a folly make.

The Spendthrift, when he takes to save, a Miser oft becomes,
   And, where he squander'd thousands once, will make his meal of crumbs.
The niggardly, when he the part of liberal would play,
   Is generous beyond his means, to give, to lend, or pay.
But both are in excess, and act in opposition quite
   To Sense and Reason's rules for doing e'en the thing that's right.
So be advised by me, my friends, and keep within the mean;
   The path of Light, the line of Right, lies all extremes between.

POR Medio y no caerey.

Allez par le Milieu, et vous ne tomberez.

——Medio tutissimus ibis.

Il n'y a banquet que de chiches.

TOO MUCH BREAKS THE BAG.

Zu wenig und zu viel
Verderbet alle Spiel.
Zu viel ist ungesund.

Al zu scharf macht schärtig.

Il, molto e'l poco.
Rompe le giuoco.

Ni tan hermosa que mate,
Ni tan fea que espante.
Ni tant belle, qu'elle tue;
Ni tant laide, qu'elle espourente.

Noch y i noch fy.

Oono bel givoco vuol duras poco.
Tien la Strada di mezzo.

Pleos viâ mediâ: medium tenuêre beati.

Qui commence à être libéral, devient prodigue.

Baullu curium etion vetra mensuras carnadu.—*Turkish Adage.*

Omnis intemperantia est a tota mente ac a recta ratione defectio.—Cicero.

Incidit in Scyllam cupiens vitare Charybdim.—*Latin Proverb.*

In arbitror adprime in vita esse utile "*ne quid nimis.*"—Terence.

Avoid Extremes.

'Tis all in vain to keep a constant pother
About one Vice, and fall into another;
Betwixt excess and famine lies a mean;
Plain, but not sordid; though not splendid, clean.—Pope.

Never exaggerate.

THE Wise never speak in the superlative, for that mode of speech always offends either Truth or Prudence. Exaggerations are so many prostitutions of reputation, inasmuch as they expose the shallowness of the understanding and the bad taste of the speaker. Exaggeration is a species of lying; he who exaggerates shews himself to be a man of bad taste, and, what is worse, a man of mean intellect.—Gracian.

MY Light into a snuffe is almost turn'd,
  And now the candle to smoaking ashes burn'd,
Behold another Light stands ready by,
Which to enjoy my place will make me dye.
Yet not unpunish'd it puts out my breath,
My very ashes doe revenge my death.

  So doth the sonne his Father make away,
  If not with sword, with griefe, before his day,
  That he his Fathers goods and meanes may joy,
  Which Nemesis revenging doth convoy.
  For oft the spendthrifts goods so evill gotten
  Are spent before his Fathers bones are rotten.

FARLIE's *Emblems*.

DO BUSINESS, BUT BE NOT A SLAVE TO IT.

When the Wind serves, all aid.

GREASE THE FAT SOW!

" WHO claimeth kindred with the Poor?"
 So few! that 'twas the reason why
The queſtion was firſt put, no doubt,—
 And truly! it doth much imply.
Replete with meaning are thoſe words,
 Though few—to picture and expreſs
In time of yore, as even now,
 Man's all-abſorbing ſelfiſhneſs.

ADVERSITY TRIES THEM.

The sage* who said in antient days:
   " When the strong-box contains no more,
And that the kitchen fire is out,
   Both friends and flatt'rers shun the door,"
Attested then, what even now
   Is daily seen on every hand:
The prosperous in life, alone
   Have proffer'd service at command.
Let Fortune with propitious winds
   Waft but the laden bark to shore,
He finds a host of helping friends,
   Who never had a friend before.
Beyond his need on ev'ry side,
   He sees unask'd-for sympathy;
Officious zeal to help and aid
   The tide of his prosperity.
" Grease the fat fowl! all help! all aid!"
   On ev'ry hand the harpies cry;
'Tis easy rowing in the wake
   Of others' toil and industry!

Thus 'tis in life, we constant see
   The Drones and Idlers of our kind,
Prey on the labours of the Bee,
   And fatten on what others find:
The Foxes of the human race,
   The Beavers of their own despoil;
Craft, lord it in poor Merit's place,
   And take the credit of his toil.

— —

Donec eris felix, multos numerabis amicos:
   Tempora si fuerint nubila, solus eris.
Aspicis ut veniant ad candida tecta columbae,
   Accipiat nullas sordida turris aves!

* Plutarch.

Horrea formicæ tendunt ad inania nunquàm :
Nullus ad amissas ibit amicus opes.
Utque comes radios per solis euntibus umbra est :
Cùm latet hic pressus nubibus, illa fugit :
Mobile sic sequitur fortunæ lumina vulgus :
Quæ simul inductâ nube teguntur, abit.—OVID, i *Trist.* 8.

GRANARO vuoto formica non frequenta.—*Italian Proverb.*

OF ledige solders en komen geen Kalanders.—*Dutch Proverb.*

WER da liegt, über dem muß alle Welt hin.—*German Proverb.*

PARENTE con parente
Guai à chi non ha niente.

VRIENDEN zijn vrienden, maer wee diese van doen heeft.

A bon vent chaque mincs side.

IN horsa serrais, amico non si trova.

VRIENDEN in der nood
Vier-en-twintigh in een lood.

FELICIUM omnes consanguinei.

MEN kent geen vrient als in der nood ;
Den rijcken na den dood.

DIEWEIL die Henn' Eier legt, legt man ihr zach.—*Old German Proverb.*

While the Pot boils, Friendship blooms.

In Prosperity Friends are numerous and cheap.

INFELICIUM nulli sunt affines.

L'HOMME pauvre est toujours en pais étranger.—JUAN RUFO, *Apoph.* 541.

THE Vulgar find Friends neither in Prosperity nor Adversity : because in the former they know nobody, and that in Adversity nobody will know them.—GRACIAN.

INTEREST makes all seem Reason that leads to it.—DRYDEN, *Sov. Love.*

THE noblest Friendship ever shown,
The Saviour's history makes known,
    Though some have turned and turned it :
And whether being crazed or blind,
Or seeking with a biassed mind,
    Have not, it seems, discerned it.—COWPER.

WHILST I did ſhine fierce Boreas put me out,
　　Againe he kindles me at the ſecond bout :
As ſometimes did the clowne, now Boreas doth,
Both heat and cold he breatheth from his mouth,
　　The billow whom it caſt into the maine,
　　Returning threw him in the Shippe againe ;
　　Fortune throwes downe, then raiſeth from the ground ;
　　Achilles ſpeare doth cure whom it did wound.
　　I ofſes prove good to ſome ; whom Greece condemnd,
　　The Perſian for his vallour could commend.
　　Be not caſt downe, diſpaire not at miſchance,
　　God who hath croſſed thee, will thee advance.

　　　　　　　　　　　　　　FARLIE'S *Emblems.*

ALTERO EXTINGUOR.

ALTERO ASCENDOR.

WHEN A MAN'S COAT IS THREADBARE,

IT IS AN EASY THING TO PICK A HOLE IN IT.

Faites feste au chien, il te gastera ton habit.

PLAY WITH THE DOG, AND HE'LL SPOIL YOUR CLOTHES.

A S in the garden yeſterday,
  In full Court ſuit, I coax'd our Tray,
  And with each friendly pat and ſtroke,
The uſual words of kindneſs ſpoke;
He in return for my careſs,
Sprang up, unmindful of my dreſs,

95

And with his dirty feet and nose
Besmear'd my handsome cloak and hose.
In spite of all that I could say,
To keep in bounds his ruthless play ;—
Grown bolder still, the vexing brute,
As though intent to spoil my suit,
Jump'd up again—my shoe-ties soil'd,
My satin knee-bows fray'd and spoil'd ;
Till finding all my chiding vain,
His wanton fondness to restrain;
In wrath I kick'd th' unmanner'd hound,
And laid him sprawling on the ground.
As with the brute, with man no less,
The friendship of th' uncultur'd mind
Is irksome oft, from sheer excess
Of zeal to do the thing that's kind.
However friendly you may be
Dispos'd your serving-man to treat,
Let not your partiality
Be shewn beyond the bound that's meet:
With equal care your fondness shew,
When you your child or dog caress;
For both alike as little know,
How far the friendship may transgress,
That ruffles self-love through the Dress.

BURLAOS con el asno, daros ha en la barba con el rabo.
   Cria corvo, y sacar te hal el ojo.—*Old Spanish Proverb.*

Las enfans et serviteurs il ne les faut mignarder, si tu veux en jouir.

FAITES feste au chat, il vous sautera au visage.
Nimia familiaritas parit contemptum.
Il troppo conversar partorisce dispregio.

Nulli te facias nimis sodalem.
Gaudebis minha? Et minks dolebis.—MARTIAL.

JAMAIS trop compagnon à nul ne te feras:
Car bien que moins de joye, moins d'ennuy tu auras.

WILL WHISK HIS TAIL IN YOUR FACE.

Chose accoustumée
N'en pas fort prisée.

A casa de tu tia,
Mas no cada dia :
A caso de tu hermano,
Non iras cada serano.

A la maison de ta tante,
Mais pas tous les jours :
A la maison de ton frère ;
Mais non tous les soirs.

Ale luporum catulos.

IN cos qui lethantur ab iis, de quibus bene meriti sint, aut in ingratos. Nam plerunque solet id usu venire illis, qui catulos luporum enutriunt.—ERASM. *in Adagns.*

Qui se fait brebis, le loup le mange ;
Qui se fait porceau, se met dans la fange :

Amignotte ton enfant, et il te donnera maint effroy :
Joue toi avec lui, et il te contristera.

Ne te joue point avec un homme mal appris.

IN reverse sense of what has been said above, the Hebrew proverb saith, " If your friend be sugar you must not eat him all up," *i.e.* that we must not require too much of those who are willing to serve us ; that we should never misuse any one's courtesy ; nor over-ride a willing horse :

SHOULD any ask the reason why
   I use nor whip nor spurs to ply
The mare I ride !—It is that she
Requires nor whip nor spur from me :
Because her mettle is so good,
And she's so willing in her mood,
That since I've her bestrode, I ne'er
Found her dispos'd her legs to spare.
For whip or spur no use I see
Whene'er a horse goes willingly :
And this I hold :—From horse nor man
That willing gives, take all you can :
Nor is he wise who tries his friend
Beyond his will to give or lend.
Who overloads his ass, no less
   T' obtain his wish the worst way chooses :
His ass stands still from sheer distress,
   And greed of gain the market loses !

NOW Boreas puffing in his boiſtrous ire,
　　Blows as he were to kindle Vulcans fire:
He doth undoe me by his churliſhneſſe,
I am confumed more, and ſhine the leſſe:
He ſpends his labour, ſo I loſe mine oyle,
As no wayes fit to undergoe ſuch toyle.

　　You beat the Aſſe ling'ring under his load,
　　The generous Horfe deſerveth not a goad:
　　The Mufes ſonnes cannot away with laſhes,
　　Which are more fitting for Arcadian aſſes.
　　Each ſtrength within his limits, Nature bounds,
　　Which who ſo paſſeth, Nature he confounds.

　　　　　　　　　　　FARLIE's *Emblems.*

THE CHILD MAY BE ROCKED TOO HARD.

Turpe Senilis Amor.

BEES TOUCH NO FADING FLOWERS.

THE Rose round which of late in fuch difport,
So many came t' admire and to court;
With drooping head now mourns that fhe fhould be
By all forfaken fhe was wont to fee.
No gentle Zephyr now as yefter-noon,
Comes near to revel in her fweet perfume;

THE FADED ROSE NO SUITOR KNOWS.

No Butterfly with wings of varied hue,
Now hovers near, and stays his flight to view
Her full-blown beauties—nor as hitherto,
To kiss from off her breast the pearly dew:
No tuneful Bee* now hies on eager wing,
His admiration of her charms to sing,
Nor longer seeks to rifle and to sip
The honied treasures of her fragrant lip.
And why is this?—the reason soon is told:
Nor Butterflies nor Bees are grown more cold—
But thou, poor Rose!—'tis thou art growing old!
Thy beauties in their prime but yesterday;—
To-day, alas! are fading fast away!
Yield thee to Love, sweet youth, while youth is thine;
Seek thee a mate e'er yet thy youth decline,
Nor make delay to love, to woo and wed,
Till Age has strewn its snows upon thine head.
Of Life's best years waste not the richest bloom
In fruitless use, for Time is Beauty's tomb;—
Youth, Strength, and Beauty have not long to stay,
To-day they're thine—to-morrow pass'd away!

AMARE juveni fructus, crimen seni—Senec. in Proverb.

 Desine, dulcium
 Mater sæva Cupidinum,
 Circà lustra decem flectere mollibus
 Tam durum imperiis. Abi
 Quò blandæ juvenum te revocant preces.—Horace.

In Caducum Parietem non inclinandum.

WHEN the fresh rose first opens to the day,
 'Tis wooed by all that love round flowers to play:
But when it droops and all its bloom is o'er,
No Bee then seeks it for its honey more.

* Aper à mansilis floribus abstinere solent : mortuis, ait Plinius, floribus ne golden corpuscles insilant

So fares it ever with the rich and great
To poverty reduc'd by adverse Fate:
Few know them then, or their acquaintance boast;
Not even those who fawn'd on them the most,
Smil'd when they smil'd, and made without a cause
Each look and word their subject for applause;
In sordid worship of that wealth and state
Which grov'lling minds then pay towards the great.
Then like the Rose deserted by the Bee,
When all its wealth of sweets has pass'd away,
Each shuns the fall'n, nor merit more can see
In him whose call they truckl'd to obey.

MY lovers and my friends stand aloof from my sore; and my kinsmen stand afar off.—*Psalm* xxxviii. 11.

MANY will entreat the favour of the prince, and every man is a friend to him that giveth gifts; [But] all the brethren of the poor do hate him: how much more do his friends go far from him!—*Prov.* xix. 6, 7.

SOME friend is a companion at the table, and will not continue in the day of thy affliction. In thy prosperity he will be as thyself, and will be bold over thy servants: [But] if thou be brought low, he will be against thee, and will hide himself from thy face.—*Ecclesiasticus* vi. 10—12.

A FRIEND cannot be known in prosperity, and an enemy cannot be hidden in adversity. In the prosperity of a man enemies will be grieved, but in his adversity even a friend will depart.—*Ibid.* xii. 8, 9.

WEALTH maketh many friends; but the poor is separated from his neighbour.
Prov. xix. 4.

THERE is a companion which rejoiceth in the prosperity of a friend, but in the time of trouble will be against him. There is a companion which helpeth his friend for the belly, and taketh up the buckler against the enemy.—*Ecclesiasticus* xxxvii. 4, 5.

WHERE the carcase is, there the eagles will be gathered together.—*Matt.* xxiv. 28.

Cum Fortuna manet vultum servatis amici,
Cum cedit, turpi vertitis ora fuga.—OVID.

RICH MEN HAVE NO FAULTS.

(left margin, vertical) PYLADES AND ORESTES DIED LONG AGO,

(right margin, vertical) AND LEFT NO SUCCESSORS.

WHEN as my Light much like an ev'ning ſtarre,
    Did caſt his glittering beames both neare and farre;
Then light me glorious, flame me dreadfull made,
And none injuriouſly durſt me upbraide;
But when my Light into a ſnuffe did turne,
And cloth'd with darkneſſe, I did ceaſe to burne,
Loe how without defence I naked ſtand,
Thus torne and rent by this devouring hand.

    Glory, as envy, ſo it terrour lends
    To Mortals: Majeſty It ſelfe defends;
    But after treacherous Fortune flies away,
    To an unarmed dwarfe its made a prey.

                  FARLIE's *Emblems.*

WHEN THE TREE IS FALLEN, EVERY ONE GOETH TO IT WITH HIS HATCHET.

THE DOG WAGS HIS TAIL NOT FOR YOU, BUT FOR THE BREAD.

ONE ILL EXAMPLE SPOILS MANY GOOD.

Pomme pourrie gâte sa compagnie.

ONE ROTTEN EGG SPOILS THE WHOLE PUDDING.

ONE ILL WEED MARS A WHOLE POT OF POTTAGE.

ONE ROTTEN APPLE INFECTS ALL IN THE BASKET.

FAIR Maid! who comes fo oft this way,
　　Your fruit of me to buy!
In guerdon of your kindnefs, pray!
　　Before my fruit you try,—
Give ear to what I have to fay,
　　For I would fervice do
To fuch as buy of me to-day,
　　Good cuftomers like you!

Full many years have I fold fruit,
  And well its nature know;
As that of ev'ry herb and root,
  That in the garden grow;—
And this I've found, and heard it too
  From all who fruit have grown,—
" However fine and frefh to view,
  The good, keep beft alone."
No rotten pear, however flight
  The token of decay,
But foon as e'er it meets the fight,
  It fhould be thrown away:
For be the damage e'er fo fmall,
  In little time, I've known
The taint will often fpread to all,
  From that one pear alone.
I've had of Jargonels a lot,
  As found as fruit could be,
All from one apple take the rot,
  And prove fad lofs to me.
Nor is there fruit that ever grew,
  When fpoiled in any part,
But foon fpoils all that's near it too,
  So take thefe truths to heart:
A tainted grape the bunch may fpoil;
  A mildew'd ear, the corn in fhock;
A fcabby fheep, with rot and boil,
  Infect and kill the fineft flock.
Hence, maiden, I would have you know
The ill that evil contact brings
To all the fineft fruits that grow,
And faireft maids, like other things.
Seek only all that's good to learn;
Thine ears from evil counfel turn;—
For all the more the fruit is fair,
The greater is its need of care.

TELL ME THE COMPANY YOU KEEP,

GUICCIARDINI, in his Book entitled "Hours of Recreation," says that it is a singular and sure way to acquire a knowledge of the inner nature and character of a person, if one diligently observes the kind of society he most frequently keeps:

> For two of a kind, whate'er they be,
> Are forthwith certain to agree:

as Cicero said formerly when speaking of Cato: because Nature always inclines to its like; and hence, specially applicable to the foregoing subject is the Spanish proverb:

> Di me con quien iras
> Dirir te he lo que haras.
>
> Tell me, with whom thou goest,
> And I'll tell thee what thou doest.

To shun evil company is therefore one of the most important things to be impressed on the mind of the youth of both sexes; and the extent of mischief which it leads to, may be well inferred from the writings of David, a man after God's heart, and of Solomon, the wisest of kings; both of whom gave this subject the first place in their writings. David in his first Psalm, and Solomon in the first chapter of his Proverbs, coincide with the sense expressed in the Proverbs of all nations, as may herein be seen:

> He that handles pitch shall foul his fingers.
>
> > Handelt gy't peck,
> > Gy krygt een vleck.
> >
> > Baldis rogneuse
> > Fait l'autre tigneuse.
>
> One rotten sheepe wille marre a whole flocke.
>
> > La manzana podrida
> > Pierde a su compania.
>
> Unica prava pecus inficit omne pecus.
> Dum spectant lesos oculi, læduntur et ipsi.—Ovid.
>
> ——— Grex totus in agris
> Unius scabie cadit, et porrigene porci:
> Uvaque conspectá livorem ducit ab uvā.—Juvenal, Sat. 2.
>
> Wer unter den Wölfen ist, muss mit ihnen heulen.
> Ein reudig Schaf macht die ganze Heerde reudig.
>
> Ein schurft schaep maeckt'er veel.
> Die by de kreupelen woont, leert hincken.
> Vuyle gronden bederven de Kabels.
>
> > Die met den goeden omme gact,
> > En acht ick noyt myn leven quaet.

FLAME goes to heav'n, from whence it once did come,
  Bids earth adue, and what it hath therefrom.
The fnuffe to afhes, fmoake turnes into ayre;
Light's beauty's gone, which fometime was fo faire;
When Death had giv'n his laft and fatall blow,
Our foule to Heav'n, our Earth to earth doth goe;
Riches and honours, which it once did love,
The Soule now lothes; and feekes to dwell above.
Learne, Mortals, all falfe pleafures to contemne,
And treafures, which the foule muft once condemne:
Seeke rather for the graces of the minde,
Which you your convoy to the Heaven will finde.

FARLIE'S *Emblems.*

Tangor, non Frangor, ab undis.

LIP WORSHIP DON'T REACH THE HEART.

PARLER DE BOUCHE, AU CŒUR NE TOUCHE.

I AM TOUCHED, NOT BROKEN BY THE WAVES.

AT ev'ry feſtive board th' admir'd gueſt,
   At ev'ry Ball the partner in requeſt ;
    'Mid Faſhion's throng wherever thou art ſeen,
Th' acknowledg'd faireſt type of Beauty's Queen :
And yet—with all this tribute to thy grace,
This fervent homage of thy form and face ;
  Unmov'd, unchang'd, thou art in all the ſame
  'As heretofore ;—nor Love, nor praiſe, nor blame,

ALLE AANSPREKERS, GEEN HERTE-BREKERS.

To thee or pleasure or annoy impart—
Such is the icy coldness of thine heart!
That thou art thus, explains full well to me,
What I once deem'd mere fabulous to be:
That even 'midst the Ocean's rolling wave,
Where all earth's waters find a common grave;
There flow some Rivers which no less maintain
Their course unbroken, and unmix'd retain
Their Water's sweetness 'mid the briny main!—[*]
So thou, who kindlest in all hearts, desire,
Mov'st cold and still unscath'd amid'st the fire!

———

QUIS fornacem Regis Babylonii sine adustione ingressus est, inquit, cujus adolescentia Ægyptica Domina pallium non terruit? Inter illecebras voluptatum etiam ferreas mentes libido domat. Difficile inter opulas servatur pudicitia.—HIERON. lib. iii. *Epist.* 5.

PERICLITATUR castitas in deliciis, humilitas in divitiis, pietas in negotiis, veritas in multiloquio, charitas in hoc mundo.—BERNARD. *in quad. Serm.*

——— ....

THE rolling wheel that runneth often round,
    The hardest steel in tract of time doth tear;
And drizzling drops, that often do redound,
The firmest flint doth in continuance wear:
Yet cannot I, with many a dropping tear
And long entreaty, soften her hard heart,
That she will once vouchsafe my plaint to hear,
Or look with pity on my painful smart.
But, when I plead, she bids me play my part;
And, when I weep, she says; Tears are but water;
And, when I sigh, she says; I know the art;
And, when I wail, she turns herself to laughter.
So do I weep, and wail, and plead in vain,
While she as steel and flint doth still remain.—EDMUND SPENSER.

— —

[*] This was anciently affirmed and believed of the River Alpheus, in its course through the Sicilian Sea.

❧ PASS THROUGH, BUT MINGLE NOT. ✦

I PRYTHEE send me back my heart,
  Since I can not have thine;
For if from yours you will not part—
  Why then shouldst thou have mine?
Yet now I think on't, let it lie,
  To find it were in vain;
For thou'rt a thief in either eye
  Would steal it back again.—Sir J. Suckling.

Oh! who would love? I woo'd a Woman once,
But she was sharper than an eastern wind,
And all my heart turn'd from her, as a thorn
Turns from the sea.—Tennyson.

The fair Lauretta's eyes, so blue and bright,
Look blank and cold when I am in her sight.
Paint her not thus, kind limner! give her that
Sweet smile she wears when talking to her cat.
So shall I fondly think, whene'er I see
The beaming Portrait, that it smiles on me.—Anon.

Mediis immixtus in undis.

READER! from this our Emblem learn to be
  Th' unmingling River flowing through the sea
Of this World's brackish waters. Thou too, keep
Thy course unbroken, 'mid the briny deep
  Of all its lures, its lusts and vanity.
Though living in men's 'midst, yield not thine heart
To those who would their taint to it impart;
Lest soon commingling with the 'whelming tide
Of Passion's waves, which press on ev'ry side,
  Thy Soul's sweet waters lose their purity.

Discite in hoc mundo, suprà mundum esse; et si corpus geritis, volitet in vobis
ales interior.—Ambros. de Virg.

That ye may be blameless and harmless, the sons of God, without rebuke, in
the midst of a crooked and perverse nation, among whom ye shine as lights in
the world.—Philip. ii. 15.

And they that use this world, as not abusing it: for the fashion of this world
passeth away.—1 Corinth. vii. 31.

W HEN thou in darkeneſſe of the night didſt blaze,
    I could not without envy on thee gaze;
But when the Cyclop Titan comes in ſight,
There is no ods twixt darkeneſſe and thy light:
I doe not envy thee, although thou ſhine;
No glor' I have, nor is the glory thine.

    As lightſome bodyes doe a ſhaddow give;
    So glory without envy cannot live:
    When greater glory doth the meane ſuppreſſe,
    It likewiſe takes the envy from the leſſe.

                    FARLIE's *Emblems.*

SAYING AND DOING ARE TWO THINGS.

NONE SO DEAF AS HE THAT WILL NOT HEAR.

Vogelen van eener veeren vliegen geern t'samen.

LIKE PLAYS BEST WITH LIKE.

LIKE WELL, LIKE BUCKET.

BIRDS OF A FEATHER FLOCK TOGETHER.

WHAT! are you then in earnest, friend?
   Oh, no!—it cannot be:
It's quite impossible that you
   Should think of courting me!
Indeed you'd better take your love
   Elsewhere; for sure am I,
We are by no means suited for
   The Matrimonial tie.

You! who by all are said to be
  A roving, ruffling blade—
And I, as ev'ry body knows,
  A quiet, gentle maid.
From early youth accustom'd to
  The peaceful joys of home,
Amid the rude and bustling world
  I have no wish to roam:
In Housewif'ry and its behests,
  The greatest charm I find,
And when from these I seek relief,
  Why then with humble mind,
I read some holy book, or spin,
  And often take delight,
To imitate in 'broidery
  Some posie's colours bright:
'Tis seldom I go out to walk,
  And in the Street but rare,
Excepting to and fro from Church,
  Or when I go to bear
Some comfort to the sick and poor;
  For we are taught to give
Some share of what we have, to those
  Who labour hard to live.
But you without restraint give loose
  To passion's wilder sway;
Love feasting, wine and riot,
  And are giv'n much to play:
You know no rest, and to your mind
  No moment hath such charms,
As when the drum or trumpet shrill
  Calls all the Camp to arms.
Methinks some Trooper's daughter were
  For you a fitter bride,
Who in the Soldier's ruder life
  And habits takes a pride:
Whose eye unmov'd could look upon
  The blood-stain'd battle-field,

A UN BOITEUX, FEMME QUI CLOCHE.

Can swing a sword and trail a pike,
  Nor to the best one yield.
Who when she hears the cannon roar,
  Would stand unmov'd by fear,
And say, what others terrifies
  Is music to her ear.
Such is the Bride would suit you best,
  The Wife whom you would find
Most suited to your habits,
  And your rougher tone of mind.
Who without dread would pass her hand
  Upon your Rapier's blade,
And bid you fight until you fell,
  And 'neath the turf were laid :
But I who am a timid thing,
  Who even fear the smoke
Of Petronel and Arquebus,
  Much less the cannon's stroke;
Who see in you alone what would
  Make me much misery,
I am no ways a match for you,
  Nor are you fit for me.
Look but around and you will see
  Where'er you turn your eye,
The Birds which on the water swim,
  And those which soar on high—
All choose their mates as most beseems,
  And concord every where;
Each woos his like, as it should be,
  And like with like doth pair.
Nought can induce the Dove to take
  The Eagle for her mate,
The Partridge to the Buzzard-hawk
  Will never link her fate;
The Raven black weds not the Swan,
  'Twas not by Nature meant,
For "Like with like" alone, my friend,
  Can give the heart content.

CHACUN AVEC SON PAREIL.

THIS waxen torch is able to endure
    The winds, when Æolus puts them in ure;
It leads the way in darkneſſe of the night,
And, though the ſerene fall, it ſhewes his Light:
The candle ſtill lurks at home, and there doth ſhow
Its light, not caring how the winds doe blow,
This as the houſes joy at home doth ſtay,
The other ſtill abroad doth make his way.

    The hardy huſband from his houſe goes forth,
    Seeking to compaſſe buſineſs of worth;
    He ſailes by rockes and ſands, early and late
    He toiles, and ſeekes to purchaſe an eſtate:
    The wife at home much like a ſnaile ſhe ſits
    On hous-wifry employing all her wits:
    Ulyſſes in his travels hard did ſhift,
    Penelope at home did uſe her thrift.

                            FARLIE's *Emblems*.

MAIS ENTRE GENS DE CONTRAIRE NATURE

Ny AMOUR NI AMITIE DURE.

Mite Pyrum vel Sponte Fluit.

FRUIT RIPENS NOT WELL IN THE SHADE.

THERE IS NO WORSE FRUIT THAN THAT WHICH NEVER RIPENS.

THE RIPE PEAR FALLS READY TO THE HAND.

WOULD'ST early be succefsful in thy suit,
Nor languish long in Love's consuming flame?—
In Beauty's garden, shun the unripe fruit,
And breathe thy passion to the riper dame.
The fruit that's green clings longest to the tree,

Nor willing yields to leave the parent spray;
While that which has attain'd maturity,
Warm'd to the core beneath the sunny ray,
Yields to the touch—and quickly comes away.

——Tolle cupidinem
Immitis uvæ:
Jam te sequetur, jam protervâ
Fronte petet Lalage maritum.—Horace, lib. 2, *Car. Od.* 5.

—— Primis et adhuc crescentibus annis.
Non mentem Venus ipsa dedit.

Homo pomo similis.

LIKE unto Man whose course is nearly run,
The Apple, ripen'd by the autumn sun,
Yields to the touch, or to the slightest breath,
And falling—is the image of his Death.
But not alone in this the semblance lies
Between the Man's and Apple's destinies:
The ripe, in Age, part ready from the spray—
The green, in Youth, are torn by force away.

Un homme, une pomme.

Nos corps, comme les fruits aux arbres attachés,
Ou meurent, tombent en terre, ou verds sont arrachés.—Du Vair's *Epictetus.*

Il me semble, que la dite comparaison est propre et vive, pour exprimer la façon de mourir, et d'un robuste jouvenceau, qui est encore en la fleur de son age, et d'un bon vieil homme, qui jà va penchant vers la terre.—Du Vair.

It is said, by the Philosopher, "Omnia quæ secundum naturam sunt, sunt habenda in bonis." But all that happens to us contrary to the usual course of nature, is generally considered lamentable. Cicero, who seems to share the sentiment of Epictetus, and who borrowed from him in his book "De Senectute," expresses himself in yet more elevated and impressive terms:

Adolescentes mihi mori sic videntur, ut aquæ multitudine flammæ vis opprimitur. Senex autem, sicut sua sponte nulla vi adhibita consumtus ignis extinguitur: et quasi poma ex arboribus, cruda si sint, si velluntur; si matura et cocta, decidunt. Sicut vitam adolescentibus vis aufert, sic senibus maturitas.

Quod crudum, idem et pertinax.

THE fruit that's ripe, parts willing from the tree;
Unripe, 'tis not so willing to comply:
Who call'd by Death resists his destiny,
Proves most that he is unprepar'd to die.

IT is sad to die before the time: idle speech! Before what time? Before that prescribed by Nature! But Nature lent life to us only, without fixing the term of its withdrawal.—CICERO.

Offeramus Deo pro munere, quod pro debito teneamur reddere.

CHRYSOS. Super Matth. In.

IN the hope of a better award,
Forgetful that Life is a loan;
We but offer to God, as reward,
The Life which is His—not our own.

OUR Life is taken from us but to give
A better life wherewith in Heav'n to live;
Unquench'd our Spirit, by our body's death,
Rises refresh'd to breathe with purer breath.

THE glories of our blood and state
Are shadows, not substantial things;
There is no armour against fate,
Death lays his icy hand on kings:
  Sceptre and crown
  Must tumble down,
And in the dust be equal made
With the poor crooked scythe and spade.—SHIRLEY.

WE spend our years as a tale that is told.—Psalm xc. 9.

THE days of our years are threescore years and ten; and if by reason of strength they be fourscore years, yet is their strength labour and sorrow; for it is soon cut off, and we fly away.—Ibid. 10.

DEATH AND THE GRAVE MAKE NO DISTINCTION OF PERSONS.

DEATH HATH NOTHING TERRIBLE IN IT BUT WHAT LIFE HATH MADE SO.

WHEN firſt my light did ſhine, you lik'd me well.
    Now that is gone: you hate my loathſome ſmell;
You with prolongers made me live, and art
Preſerv'd my life; but now Time acts his part:
Triumphant Time, ſhewes now my glaſſe is runne,
(What way God knowes) I finde my threed is ſpunne;
Envy hath playd its part, and I doe goe
To Coffin: as I doe, all muſt doe ſo.
Time breaths a ſhrewd and life-bereaving blaſt,
Yet upward flyes my light, where it ſhall laſt.
I'me glad to part from body, which I lov'd
So deere, that many wayes and arts I prov'd
The mudwall to maintaine, and body ſave,
But yet in ſpite of me 'twill go to grave.
This is my comfort, Body, that thy tombe
Which is thy grave, ſhall be thy mothers wombe,
To bring thee once againe unto the light,
And life, which death ſhall never know, or night:
Then be content, though you and I depart:
Yet Soule and Body ſtill ſhall have one heart.— FARLIE's *Emblems*.

Quid non sentit amor?

WHO IS INSENSIBLE TO LOVE?

BEHOLD the wond'rous sympathy between
The strings of yonder lute, and this I play!
Is it not just as though some hand unseen
Swept the same chords, and tun'd the self-same lay? *

* The cause of this phenomenon is assigned by Cardanus in his 8th book *De Subtate.*
Du Plein, in his *Corps de Philosophie,* 1626, accounts for it also in nearly similar terms.—NOTE OF TRANSLATION

AMOR REGGE SENZA LEGGE.

So lov'd one—though untouch'd by thee, I feel,
Senſe of thy touch through all my being ſteal;
Hear thy lov'd voice though ſilent thou may'ſt be,
See thy lov'd form though far away from me,
And all the radiance of thy Beauty's light,
Undimm'd to me by diſtance, ſhines no leſs
To me effulgent in my dream of night,
As doth by day its light of lovelineſs.

———

Vetus verbum est, similitudinem amoris auctorem esse.—Plato, lib. 6, *De Leg.*

Experientiâ notum est arcanam quandam et occultam inter homines esse natu rarum affinitatem aut odium, vel naturæ quâdam occultâ vi, vel astrorum influentiâ. vel, &c. Unde fit ut aliquis ab altero toto pectore abhorreat, in alterum verò propensus sit, nec rogatus causam dicere posset cur hunc amet, illum oderit, juxtà illud Catulli,

> Non amo te, Voluſi, nec poſſum dicere quare.
> Hoc tantùm poſſum dicere, non amo te.—
> Cypr. *Tract. de Spons.* cap. 7.

Quin non cernit Amor! quid non vestigat Amator!—Bernald.

———

LOVE looks not with the eyes, but with the mind,
And therefore is wing'd Cupid painted blind;
Nor hath Love's mind of any judgment taste,
Wings and no eyes, figure unheedy haste;
And therefore is Love said to be a child,
Becauſe in choice he often is beguil'd.—Shakespeare.

Things baſe and vile, holding no quality.
Love can transpoſe to form and dignity.—*Ibid.*

Ah! I remember,—and how can I
But evermore remember well,—when firſt
Our flame began; when ſcarce we knew what 'twas,
The flame we felt; when as we ſat and ſigh'd,
And looked upon each other and conceived
Not what we ail'd, yet ſomething we did ail;
And yet were well, and yet we were not well;
And what was our diſeaſe we could not tell.—*Old Poet.*

——Love refines
The thoughts and heart enlarges: hath its seat
In reason, and is judicious: is the scale
By which to Heavenly love thou mayest ascend;—
Not sunk in carnal pleasure: for which cause
Among the beasts no mate for Love was found.·· MILTON.

Oh! there are looks and tones that dart
An instant sunshine through the heart;
As if the soul that minute caught
Some treasure it through life had sought;
As if the very lips and eyes
Predestin'd to have all our sighs,
And never be forgot again,—
Sparkled and spoke before us then.—MOORE.

Why should I blush to own I love!
'Tis love that rules the realms above!
Why should I blush to say to all,
That virtue holds my heart in thrall!
Is it weakness thus to dwell
On passion that I dare not tell?
Such weakness I would ever prove—
'Tis painful, but 'tis sweet to love.—KIRKE WHITE

Gaudendum cum Gaudentibus.
Joying with the Joyful.

A S late to lute in harmony attun'd,
    Vibrates in glad response, as though it shar'd
The joy that thrills the other's waken'd strings;
So let thine heart responsive share the joy
Thy neighbour feels; nor look with sullen eye
On eyes where gladness beams. Learn thou from this
To share in the delight which others feel,
And banish rankling envy from thy breast
When fortune smiles upon thy fellow man.——
Learn thou from this no less his grief to soothe
With brotherly response; for just as joy
Gains increase more from that which it bestows,
So grief grows less, lull'd by the soothing tones
Of Pity's kind compassion for her woes.

Thou wilt shew me the path of life: in thy presence is fulness of joy; at thy
right hand there are pleasures for evermore.—*Psalm* XVI. 11.

HERO who dwelt by Helkſponticke ſtrand,
Hang'd forth a Light, Leanders marke for land,
Whither his helmeleſſe courſe he ſteerd and mov'd,
Whilſt he made haſte to ſee his welbelov'd;
Which when fierce Boreas with his bluſtring blaſt
Put out, he in the floods away was caſt:
So that his wedding light became a torch,
To convoy him to Proſerpines blacke porch.

    Almighty God who made all by his power,
    Holds forth his Light from the Celeſtiall Tower:
    That when the ſtormes our toſſed soules annoy,
    It may direct us to our heav'nly joy.
    No ſtorme againſt this Light can ſo prevaile
    But Saints unto their wiſht-for Haven may ſaile.
    Where for their Wedding torch this Light they have,
    Which never ſhall convoy them to their grave.

                      FARLIE's *Emblems.*

Ut lapfu graviore ruant.

A GRANDE MONTÉE GRANDE DESCENTE.

A GRAN SUBIDA GRAN CAYDA.

THE HIGHER THE RISE THE GREATER
THE FALL.

A TORTOISE of ambitious mind,
  Such as in Men we fometimes find,
  Puff'd up with an egregious fenfe
Of his fuperior excellence,
Much wifh'd to change his lot on earth
Fer one more fitted to his worth;

PRIDE IS THE BEGINNING OF ALL DESTRUCTION.

123

Which in his felf-conceit he deem'd
Too little by his friends efteem'd—
Who neither would allow nor fee
That he poffefs'd a quality
Of form or of intelligence,
Beyond their Tortoife common fenfe.
Refolved ne'erlefs that they fhould be
Convinc'd of his ability,
'To fhine where they could never hope
With his fuperior mind to cope;
Seeing one day the bird of Jove
Alighting from the clouds above,
He urged him with addrefs polite
To bear him upward in his flight;
That he might prove to all his race
How qualified he was to grace
A ftation more exalted than
Their weak intelligence could fcan:
Whence he at once might grafp and fee
The glories of the land and fea,
And like the eagle gaze upon
The full effulgence of the fun,
High up above the puny ken
Of grov'lling Tortoifes and men.
The Eagle, quick as thought to fee
The filly reptile's vanity,
Exprefs'd himfelf but too content
To do what from the firft he meant:
And feizing him right quickly too,
He upward with the Tortoife flew,
So high into the realms of light,
That almoft lofing fenfe and fight,
The Tortoife wifhed himfelf again
Below upon the humble plain.
But upward ftill the Eagle rofe,
As though pretending to difclofe

A range of view as high and wide
As moſt would ſatiſfy his pride.
Like ſilver threads the rivers flow,
And wind ſome thouſand feet below:—
Like mole-hills are the mountains high—
In vaſt expanſe, Earth, ſea and ſky
Lit up and flooded with a light
Too glorious for the reptile's ſight.
Anon, the Eagle aſks him how
He liked the change from things below?
If higher yet he'd like to riſe?
And felt at home? and how the ſkies
Agreed with his abilities?
When lo! the Tortoiſe, all diſmay,
Had not a ſingle word to ſay!
With ſcornful and deriſive ſhriek,
Unlooſing then both claws and beak,
The Eagle lets the Tortoiſe go;
Which, daſh'd upon the rocks below,
Became his prey, and learnt—too late—
The ills that on ambition wait.

E'en ſo at Courts, when men of low degree,
And menial minds, are raiſed to rank and place;
How oft are they uplifted but to be
Caſt down with greater force and more diſgrace!

FORTUNA vitrea eſt ; tum, cùm ſplendet, frangitur.—P. SYRUS.

MAGNA ruunt, inflata crepant, tumefacta premuntur.—LUCAN. i. ver. 1).

——————— SUMMISQUE negatum
Stare diu, nimioque graves ſub pondere lapſus.—SYRACH. ili. 12.

SEEKEST thou great things for thyſelf? ſeek them not : for, behold, I will bring evil
upon all fleſh, ſaith the Lord.—Jer. xlv. 5.

GOD hath a ſpecial indignation at Pride, above all ſins.—BISHOP HALL.

ONE chinke there was and not another way
  For Boreas, his fury to eſſay;
So Hectors fatall gift Ajax confounded,
And ſtob'd him where he onely could be wounded;
Apollo so directed Paris dart
To wound Achilles foote, and kill his heart.
  Death lies in ambuſh like an enemy,
  And braſheth where our ſconces weakeſt be.
  Whether an iceele or drop of water,
  Or gnat, or Londons Scholler-killing letter.
  A thouſand trickes we ſee of cunning death,
  He makes or finds a way to ſtop our breath.

FARLIE's Emblems.

UNMERITED HONOURS NEVER WEAR WELL.

PRIDE AND SWEERNESS TAK MEIKLE UPHAUDING.

TO STAND UPRIGHT.

El corcobado no vee su corcova, y vee la de su companza.

THE HUNCHBACK SEES NOT HIS OWN HUMP, BUT HE SEES HIS NEIGHBOUR'S.

WITH rare exception, almost ev'ry one
    Is wondrous apt his Neighbour's faults to see;
And yet, however evident his own,
    To them he's blind—or thinks that only he
From imperfection and from fault is free.

EVERY MAN HATH A FOOL IN HIS SLEEVE.

A Hunchback here, brimfull of felf-conceit,
Derides a fellow-Hunchback paffing by;
And points to him, that ev'ry one they meet
May ridicule the man's deformity.
Yet he himfelf; the Jeerer, what is he?—
A crooked Dwarf, mis-fhap'd from head to toe,
With hofs behind of fuch enormity,
As though a mountain on his back did grow!
And what is man, that he would cenfor be
Of that which Nature gave his fellow-man!
In what deriving from ourfelves, are we
In aught entitled other men to fcan?
Shall we affume in figures of our own
To reckon up another man's account!
And carp at him for flaws and faults alone,
When our own ledger fhews no fmall amount!
To ev'ry man, we know to indicate
Wherein he fails—and—ftrange fagacity!
To make the moft unerring eftimate
Of what he is—and what he ought to be!
But on himfelf, who turns his eye? not one!
And though fo keen our neighbour's humps to fee,
We're blind to that upon our back alone,
E'en though that hump by far the greater be!
It was not thus, my friends, that we were taught
That practice fweet of Love and Charity,
By which the Man-God our Redemption bought,
In pity for our mortal frailty!
Look not in fcorn upon thy brother's fhape,
If nature chofe to vary it from thine;
For though it may refemble more the Ape,
It may have Light within far more divine!
Turn thine eyes inward on thine heart, and fee
What flaws are there, what feething germs of ill
That need thy care, left their malignity
Shall render thee one day more hideous ftill.

Who ridicules his neighbour's frailty,
Scoffs at his own in more or less degree:
Much wiser he who others' lets alone,
And tries his talent to correct his own.

AND why beholdest thou the mote that is in thy brother's eye, but considerest
not the beam that is in thine own eye!
Thou Hypocrite, first cast out the beam out of thine own eye; and then shalt thou
see clearly to cast out the mote out of thy brother's eye.—*Matt.* vii. 3, 5.

Qui d' autruy parler voudra,
Regarde moy; et il taira.

No ay quien sus foltas entienda,
Como las de su vecino.

Il n'y a personne qui reconnoît ses fautes,
Comme celles de son voisin.

Dal biasima altrui, che se stesso condanna.

Ziehe Dich selber bei der Nase.

Een ander heeft altyt de schult,
Geen mensch en siet syn eygen bult.

CRIMINA qui cernunt aliorum, nec sua cernunt,
Hi sapiunt aliis, desipiuntque sibi.—OWENUS.

THESE are those who can see the faults of others, but who cannot discern their
own.—These people are wise for others, and fools to themselves.

EST proprium stultitiæ, aliorum vitia cernere; oblivisci suorum.—CICERO.

NIHIL turpius est convitio quod in auctorem recidit.—PLUTARCH.

OF all the causes which conspire to blind
Man's erring judgment, and misguided mind,
What the weak head with strongest bias rules
Is Pride, the never-failing Vice of Fools.
                                                    POPE.

FOLLY IS PRIME COUNSELLOR.

IN vaine thou mantles up this light of mine,
   Thinking that no man fhall perceive it fhine
But all in vaine, flame will it felfe bewray,
And through thy coat, by burning, make his way.
   Who in his lower heart doth hurt conceale,
   Hoping that nothing fhall the fame reveale,
   He hides the torches of the hellifh rout,
   Which will at length with violence burft out:
   Who doth conceive Oreftes' impious thought,
   It will ere long to furious fact be brought.
   Diffemble what thou can'ft, that inward fparke
   Will burft forth into Light, though now its darke.

                FARLIE'S *Emblems.*

LES TONNEAUX VIDES SONT CEUX

QUI FONT LE PLUS DE BRUIT.

Non intrandum, aut penetrandum.

ENTER NOT, OR PASS THROUGH.

A S with the Web fpun by the Spider's care,
  T' entrap the flies and gnats which fill the air,
 So with th' entangling nets by Venus laid
T' enfnare the hearts of heedlefs youth and maid:—
For in the Love net, as the Spider's too,
The gnat is taken, but the Bee breaks through.

VOLONTE REND TOUT POSSIBLE.

Hence, young folks, learn thro' Venus' nets to break,
Nor let their flimsy meshes captive take
Both heart and mind: Take pattern by the Bee:—
Like him resist the loss of liberty;
Break boldly through; but if the strength you lack,
Take my advice, and cleverly turn back.

—

Qui trop embrasse, peu estreint.

THE Spider which too widely spreads his net
Before a door, or window's open space;
Incurs more risk his livelihood to get
Than one which chooses a more humble place.
A Horse-fly now, and now a bird breaks through,
Making vast rents, through which the flies make way;
And he, poor fool, has little else to do
Than mend his net, and fast throughout the day.
He who from failure would secure disgrace,
Must never all at once too much embrace:
Who seek to compass least, and least aspire,
Achieve most oft the things which they desire.

———

Hoc unum moneo, si quid modò creditur arti,
Aut nunquàm tentes, aut perfice.—OVID. de Art. i.

Le vice est de n'en pas sortir; non pas d'y entrer.
MICH. MONTAIGNE, Essais, lib. iii. cap. 5.

In vulnus majora patent.
Forti et fideli nihil difficile.
Possunt, quia posse videntur.—VIRGIL.

AUDACES fortuna juvat.
Camelus desiderans cornua etiam aures perdidit.
Qui totum vult, totum perdit.—PUBL. SYRUS.

Intra fortunam quisque debet manere suam.—OVID.

Mieux reculer que mal assaillir.

Pervia virtuti, sed vilibus invia.

AND that they may recover themselves out of the snare of the Devil, who are taken captive by him at his will.—2 *Timothy* ii. 26.

As in the mesh spread by the Spider's skill,
The weaker flies and gnats alone are caught,
While insects more robust of wing and will,
Break boldly through, nor heed his toils in aught:
What to the virtuous heart shall bar the way,
Or hold it from the chosen path of good!—
Since this World's snares are but as frail a stay,
And as the Spider's easily withstood,
When heart and mind with one accord unite
To force through ev'ry stop the road to Right.

Hold on thy course to Virtue, nor refrain;
The wind the chaff disperses, not the grain.

His own iniquities shall take the wicked himself, and he shall be holden with the cords of his sins.—*Proverbs* v. 22.

DIABOLUS non invalesceret contrà nos, nisi viros ex vitiis nostris præberemus, et locum ei dominandi nobis peccato faceremus: unde nolite locum dare diabolo.

AUGUST. *Hom.* 3.

Cuore forte
Rompe cattiva sorte.

Vaine peur certaine misère.

Een moedig hert
Vermint de smert.

Beter is't te rug gegaen
Als een quaden sprong gedaen.

He that begins without reason, hath reason enough to leave off, by perceiving he had no reason to begin.—J. TAYLOR, vol. xii. p. 28.

EVERY MAN IS THE ARCHITECT OF HIS OWN FORTUNE.

I SHINED brightly whilſt I ſtood upright,
  And firmely ſeated gave a perfect light;
But after that miſchance did me ſurpriſe,
I am caſt downe and know not how to riſe.
Helpe, helpe, who ſees my caſe, now ſuccour me,
So, as before, my Light ſhall glorious be.

  A man may fall, this brittle life of ours
  Is ſubject to more chances than to houres:
  Or fortune falſe, or errours ſlippery fall,
  Suffers us not, conſtant to proove at all:
  Happy is he who falling findes a man,
  Much like a God, ſupporting what he can.
  By hurt he learning gaines, he wiſer growes,
  And with the weary Oxe more warily goes.

                              FARLIE's *Emblems.*

PRUDENCE WILL THRIVE WHERE GENIUS WILL STARVE.

WE READILY BELIEVE WHAT WE WISH.

Ein klein Henn leget alle Tag, da ein Strauss im Jahr nur eins.

LITTLE WINNING MAKS A HEAVY PURSE.

LITTLE AND OFTEN FILLS THE PURSE.

A HEN LAYS EVERY DAY,
BUT AN OSTRICH ONLY ONCE A YEAR.

HEAR now what has befallen me; I'm nicely taken in!
All through my Wife! who thought at once a mine of wealth to win:
A Dealer shew'd this Ostrich and its egg to her one day,
And making her believe 'twas such a wondrous bird to lay;
I bought it at her bidding—brought it home, and, like her, thought
A Bird that lay such eggs as that, could not be dearly bought.

A PASSO A PASSO SE VA LONTANA.

Hens' eggs (thought I), however good, were at the best but small,
And, as compar'd to Ostrich eggs, were of no size at all.
Off such an egg as that, why, two could make a dinner quite,
'Twas big enough to satisfy a ploughman's appetite.
Such was my mind: but very soon I'd reason to regret
I'd parted with my money, or an Ostrich ever met.
It eat! Oh! such a bird to eat as that I never saw!
No end of food and things could satisfy its hungry maw;
But Eggs! not one it laid! though all the while I did my best
With hay and straw and feathers soft to make the bird a nest.
When, after waiting long,—'twas just about the month of May—
I found one egg! Eh! now, thought I, it has begun to lay!
But all my joy was very short, for from that time till now,
It hasn't laid another egg, nor will it any how.
Yet all this while our Hens, as is with Hens the usual way,
They've always laid at intervals, and often ev'ry day.
At length, all patience losing, and my temper put about,
I went up to the Ostrich, and I call'd to him; Turn out!
Away with you, you rav'nous brute, you shall no longer stay!
You're big enough, and eat enough, and yet no eggs you lay.
I see how 'tis with you, you're all appearance, nothing more;
In buying you I've learnt what I ought well t' have known before:
The biggest things are not the best, the brightest often dross;
And when we grasp at profit most, we oft get greater loss.

A PIUMA à piuma se pela l'oca.
A gotta à gotta il mar si seccherebbe.

Von kleinen Fischlein werden die Hechte gross.

Peu à peu file la vieille sa quenouille.

Qui s'aglie, s'enrichit.

Little pot, soon hot.

Il bue s'è fatto grande, e la stalla piccola.
The ox fattens in a little stall.

En petite maison Dieu a grand part.

FORTUNAM qui avidè vorare petgit,
Hanc tandem male concoquat necesse est.

CELUI qui méprise les petites choses, tombera peut à petit.—*Syrach.* xxiv. 1.

LE peu est suffisant à l'homme bien appris.—*Ib.* xxx. 21.

KLEYN visje, soet visje.

Majora petiles, parva ni servaveris.
Who neglects the little, loses the greater.

ADDE parum parvo, tandem fit magnus acervus.
Gutta cavat lapidem.—OVID.

WER keinen Pfennig achtet,
Der auch nimmer eines Gulden Herre.

ALEAXANSE los adarves,
Y alcanse los muladeres.

MET veel slagen wort de Stockvisch murw.

GRANO à grano hinche la gallina el papo.
Grain à grain
Amasse la fourmy son pain.

DOET by een kleyntje dikmaels wat,
Soo wort'et noch een groote schat.

DIIS proximus est, quicunque eget paucissimus.

Tandem fit Surculus Arbor.

HOW small soe'er your Profit be,
    Despise it not, but learn to know.
That almost ev'ry thing you see
    From small at first to large did grow:
Do but a little oft, and you
    Will find that little grow apace;
The Penny to the Pound accrue,
    And "slow and sure oft win the race."

THAT LITTLE WHICH IS GOOD FILLS THE TRENCHER.

THE Smith, the steele so tempers in the fire,
  As that it may indure flints stroke and ire;
The flint and steele, 'gainst other while they strive,
Give sparkles, which the tinder keeps alive,
Untill the sulphure to the match gives flame,
Which keeps, and to the candle doth give the same;
The candle thus lighted proper use hath none:
Thus all ordained is for man alone.
    Dame Nature so commandeth ev'ry thing
    In his owne kind to serve his Lord and King;
    Things of meere being, and which doe not live,
    As Elements, food to the living give;
    The living herbs doe beasts with sense mainetaine
    And these, to feede us, ev'ry houre are slaine:
    So every thing is for the use of man,
    To God should he not doe then, what he can!
                              FARLIE'S *Emblems*.

Verwonnen Oog, begonnen Min.

THE EYE IS BLIND IF THE MIND IS ABSENT.

CIECO E L'OCCHIO, SE L'ANIMO E DISTRATTO.

WHEN THE EYES ARE WON, LOVE IS BEGUN.

’TWAS faid of Old,—and, like moſt ſayings too,
It hath been proven by experience true,
That e’en defpite his fierce majeſtic might,
“Who wins the Lion’s eyes, subdues him” quite.
Herein is well explain’d and typified
Another truth that cannot be denied:
The eye of Man once taken by the grace
And ’witching beauty of a Maiden’s face,

ŒIL GAGNE, CORPS PERDU.

However ftern his nature hitherto,
Affumes a foftnefs it before ne'er knew.
Ah! then how chang'd the cold imperious look
That scarce the gaze of other eyes could brook!
How pliant then the ftemly moulded mind
Of Sage and Soldier, as of rugged hind!
Each then alike, as though himfelf defpite,
Submits his ruder to the gentler might;
And, Strength to Softnefs through the eyes betray'd,
The Lion, gentle as the Lamb is made.

———

NON benè conveniunt, nec in unâ sede morantur
   Majestas et Amor.—OVID, *Metam.* 3.

QUISQUIS amat, servit; sequitur captivus amatam,
Fert domitâ cervice jugum, fert dulcia tergo
Verbera, fert stimulos, trahit et bovis instar aratrum.—MANTUAN.

Par des yeux les deux fenestres,
Dards d'Amour deviennent maistres.

PRIMI, in omnibus proeliis, oculi vincuntur.—TACIT. *de Morib. Germ.*

CLAMOR repentinus aliquis, aut imago, aut aspectus fugâ sæpè exercitum implevit; et hæc talia magis, quàm gladius, consternant hostem, videbisque militem vanis et inanibus magis, quàm justis formidinis causis moveri.—LIPS. *Dict. Civil.* lib. v. cap. 16.

NIHIL tam leve est, quod non magnæ interdum rei momentum faciat.

LES Femmes peuvent tout, parce qu'elles gouvernent les personnes qui gouvernent tous.

———I HAVE mark'd
A thousand blushing apparitions
To start into her face, a thousand innocent shames,
In Angel whiteness, bear away those blushes;
And in her eye there hath appear'd a fire
To burn the errors that these princes hold
Against her maiden truth.—SHAKESPEARE.

BEAUTY with a bloodless conquest finds
A welcome sov'raignty in rudest minds.—WALLER.

———

——Whose radiant look strikes every gazing eye
Stark blind, and keeps th' amaz'd beholder under
The stupid tyranny of Love and wonder.—*Old Poet.*

Then only hear her Eyes;
Tho' they are mute, they plead, nay, more, command:
For beauteous Eyes have arbitrary power.—Dryden.

Who knows how eloquent these Eyes may prove,
Begging in Floods of Tears and Flames of Love.—Roch.

The Bloom of op'ning Flowers, unsully'd Beauty,
Soften and sweetest Innocence she wears;
And looks like Nature in the World's first spring.—Rowe.

- - -

Nequitiæ Ducti, Oculi.

The Light of the Body is the Eye: therefore when thine eye is single, thy whole
body also is full of light; but when thine eye is evil, thy body also is full of dark-
ness. Take heed therefore that the Light which is in thee be not darkness.—*Luke*
xi. 34, 35.

But if thine Eye be evil, thy whole Body shall be full of Darkness. If therefore
the Light that is in thee be Darkness, how great is that Darkness!—*Matt.* vi. 23.

- - -

Love in the Godhead.

FOR Love it was, that first created Light,
  Mov'd on the Waters, chac'd away the Night
From the rude Chaos, and bestow'd new Grace
On Things dispos'd of to their proper Place;
Some to rest here, and some to shine Above:
Earth, Sea, and Heav'n were all th' Effects of Love.—Wall.

Love is that Passion, which refines the Soul;
First made Men Heroes, and those Heroes Gods:
Its genial fires inform the sluggish Mass;
The rugged soften, and the am'rous warm.
Give Wit to Fools, and Manners to the Clown;
The rest of Life is an ignoble Calm;
The Soul, unmov'd by Love's inspiring breath,
Like lazy Waters, stagnates and corrupts.—Hig. *Gen. Con.*

MY splendor with his bright and Sun-like ray,
 Doth cheere the houfe, and darkeneffe chafe away:
To thee wh' art blind, I'm dark as fable night,
It's thy default, not mine, thou lik'ft thy fight.
The Moule cannot Hyperions glory fee;
Who want their eyes, no comfort have by me.
    Chrift is the glory of that light from hie,
    Which can the darkeft Chaos full defcry;
    And yet we fee him not untill our eyes
    He open, which thickeft darkeneffe doth furprife;
    Then doth his light unto himfelfe reflect
    From us as mirrours, with a new afpect.
                                FARLIE's *Emblems.*

Snijt men fin Neus af, men cheut fijn Aenficht.

WHO CUTS OFF HIS NOSE SPITES HIS OWN FACE.

COME here, all Friends, who know, and would
    Advife me for the beft;—
I've got a Nofe, the fight and thought
    Of which deftroys my reft.
A Nofe, alas! with wens and wheals
    Surcharged and cover'd o'er;
A huge unfightly Nofe, fuch as
    No man e'er had before.

THAT GOOD MAY COME.

143

It looks juſt like a bald-coot's noſe,
It's ſcarlet-red and blue,
And juſt as if a younger lot
Of Noſes on it grew.
Oh, ſuch a Noſe! a ſnout ſo ſtrange!
That when I'm in the ſtreet,
Each looks at it ſurpris'd, and all
The children that I meet
Point after me and ſay, "Oh! what
A Noſe that man has got!
Who ever ſaw the like of that?
'Tis like a Porter's knot!"
And in forſooth, my Noſe is like
An Oſtrich-egg in ſize,
'Tis like a huge black-pudding that
Stands out between my eyes.
At ſight of it, myſelf, ſometimes
I'm terrified, nor know
What with it I'm to do, or if
Yet larger it may grow.
A Noſe!—but there, I've ſaid enough;
I cannot longer bear
So hideous a thing as this
Upon my face to wear.
I often think I'll cut it off!—
And why not?— why delay
To do what one hears ſpeak of in
The Proverb ev'ry day?
But hold! are Noſes after all
No uſe upon the face?
Although their ſhape and ſize be not
Conſiſtent quite with grace?
If cut it off I do—Why what
An awful gap there'll be!
Without a Noſe, my face will then
Be horrible to ſee!
Eh! friend, put by thy knife, nor lift
A ſuicidal hand
Againſt thyſelf! for as thou art,
'Tis meet to underſtand,
Lies neither in thy will nor right

To mar, nor to upbraid;
　Bow meekly rather to His Will
　　Who thine affliction laid!
Seek not with violence to do
　What patience may effect;
By gentle means 'tis easier oft
　To heal and to correct.
Try these, my friend, they may avail,
　But should they not succeed,
Spare thine own flesh, nor mar thy face
　By such ungodly deed.
Wouldst further know, my friends, some rule
　Of conduct to deduce
From this my theme? Read on—my aim
　Is but to be of use.
Herefrom learn also to respect
　The failings of thy friend,—
To him who to thy blood belongs,
　Thine helping hand extend:
When husband or the wife have left
　Their duty's path awhile—
A mother, brother, sister err'd,
　Strive thou to reconcile.
Forsake thy kindred not that they
　Have fall'n their cross beneath;
The strength has not been giv'n to all
　To gain the Victor's wreath:
Though thou their errors mayest hate,
　Let judgment be deferr'd;
Hate thou not them, but pity more
　That they should so have err'd.
Drag not their faults into the light,
　But kindly draw the veil,
As teaches Love, that other eyes
　May see not where they fail.
Be the Physician thou, and strive
　All that thou canst to cure;
Canst thou not heal, then learn, and teach
　How others may endure.
The suff'ring limb by force is not made whole,
Nor heals Reproof the gangrene of the soul.

CHARITY SHALL COVER THE MULTITUDE OF SINS.

MY Light is pleafant, when the night doth gloome,
　　And pitchy darkeneſſe lines the mourning roome;
Whither thou liſts Cleanthes ſmoake to blow,
Or if the Matron like to twiſt her tow.
When Phœbus ſetteth, I watch centenall
Untill he from my ſtation doth me call.

　Spare me, lend not my light to Titans ray;
　So ſhalt th' enjoy me when there is no day.
　If thy eſtate be meane, huſband it well,
　And it Attalick wealth ſhall parallell.

FARLIE's *Emblems.*

HE THAT FOLLOWETH MERCY FINDETH LIFE.

BE YE KIND ONE TO ANOTHER.

Nach vinnigh Slaen, noch harden Dzanck,
En brengt den Esel tot den Drank.

THOUGH TAKEN TO THE WATER'S BRINK,
NO BLOWS CAN FORCE THE HORSE TO DRINK.

I N vain with cheering words I've tried,
And ev'ry means that I can think
Of oaths, and blows, and kicks beside
To get this plaguey beast to drink!
I've led him by the bridle thrice,
And coax'd and pull'd, and coax'd again,

WHEN THE WINE IS IN, THE WIT IS OUT.

DRINK WASHES OFF THE DAUB AND DISCOVERS THE MAN.

DRINKING KINDNESS IS DRUNKEN FRIENDSHIP.

But he won't drink at any price,
    And blows and words alike are vain.
Yet when I turn the matter o'er,
    I really think, myfelf defpite,
That I in fenfe am wanting more,
    And of the two the Horfe is right!
Why, after all, fhould I feel fore
    And lofe my temper in this way?
The beaft p'rhaps drank enough before,
    And feldom drinks three times a day;
That's why he had no will thereto,
    Nor would approach the water's brink:
But how could I expect him to?
    If he'd nor thirft nor need of drink!
And if the brute himfelf but had
    The pow'r of fpeech, affuredly,
Brute as he is, he'd call me mad,
    And much the greater fool than he!
Hence it is plain that even Man,
    So bent each beaft with fcorn to treat,
May learn from them more wifdom than
    In his own fellow oft he'll meet!
For lo! no force can bring the beaft
    To drink, if not his thirft to flake,
While Man, creation's lord at leaft,
    Will drink all day for drinking's fake!
The faying is well known and true,
    That when a beaft has drank his need,
E'en though a King himfelf might fue,
    He'll drink no more, not he, indeed!
Fie! Man!—fie! you, the lord of Mind!
    Who, fway'd by fenfelefs appetite,
In needlefs drink enjoyment find,
    'Gainft nature, reafon, and 'gainft right!
Your thirft once quench'd, defift, nor let
    The taunts of fools, nor warmth of friends
Prevail to make you once forget
    The bound where Reafon's empire ends.

WHAT THE SOBER MAN HAS IN HIS HEART

DRUNKENNESS IS VOLUNTARY MADNESS.

Are you your Senfes', Paffions' flave,
  More than the humble brute a-field?
Or in the pow'r of Mind you have,
  Muft it before his Inftinct yield!
What would the people fay to fee
  Good wine into the Kennel caft?
And yet, the Drunkard, is not he
  A human Kennel to the laft?
Why good drink down the Sewers throw?
  Worfe than the brute art thou, Man-fool!
Wouldft thou a nobler duty know,
  Betake thee to the Horfe to fchool.
If 't's more than Horfes' work to think;
  In one thing yet the Horfe ftands firft,
It's more than Horfes' work to drink
  Without the need or fenfe of thirft.

Il n'eft manger, qu'à bonne faim.

A coulons souls cerises ambrea.

Jamais homme sage on vit
Buveur de vin sans appétit.

Vin dentro, sermo fuori.
Wer Wein eingehet, da gehet wiss auss.

Ne monstre pas ta vaillance à bien boire : car le vin a faict périr plusieurs.
                                                 SYRACH. xxxi. 29.

Wine measurably drunk, and in reason, bringeth gladness of heart and cheerfulness
of the mind ; but wine drunken with excess maketh bitterness of the mind—diminishes
strength, and maketh wounds.—*Ecclesiasticus* xxxi. 28, 30.
  The first glass for thirst, the second for nourishment, the third for pleasure, and
the fourth for madness.—ANACHARSIS.

As surfeit is the father of much faft.
So every scope by the immoderate use
Turns to restraint : our natures do pursue
(Like rats that raven down their proper bane)
A thirsty evil, and when we drink we die.
                                 SHAKESP. *Measure for Measure.*

WHEN Phœbus fets in the Hefperian ftreames,
  And Wefterne fhores blufh with his drowned beames;
Then I as Phœbus fecond muft give Light,
And act my part in darkeneffe of the night:
But now my Light complaines that I decay,
And into greafie teares doe melt away;
So I am forft to yeeld.   O turne thy teame
Phœbus, and Phofpher fhew thy morning beame.

      When Chrift the Sonne of righteoufneffe did goe
      Vnto his Heavenly manfions from below,
      Then he his holy fervants did command,
      Confpicuous to the world, like lights, to ftand;
      But when they faile with watching, toile, and age,
      And now are ready to goe off the ftage,
      Then up they yeeld the light of life and cry;
      O come thou Sonne of righteoufneffe, we die.

                                    FARLIE's *Emblems.*

DRUNKENNESS TURNS A MAN OUT OF HIMSELF,

NIET UYT LUST, MAER OM TE LEVEN.

Nimia libertas fit servitus.

NE QUID NIMIS.

NOTHING IN EXCESS.

EXCESS OF LIBERTY LEADS TO SERVITUDE.

U NTIL this haplefs moment I was free,
 And went where'er my will or fancy led;
But now oh! where -where is that liberty
So long my boaft? alas! for ever fled.
Ah! woe is me that ever I was lur'd
By aught fo poor and tafelefs as this rind,
To enter here, before I was affur'd
Some means of exit and efcape to find.

EXTREMES ARE EVIL.

Till now without reſtraint I ran about,
Each place alike, a houſe ſecure for me;
I'd holes in plenty to go in and out,
Nor fear'd our race's direſt enemy.
Now here, now there, the barn, the granary,
The kitchen, larder, parlour, and the ſtore
Were mine to roam in full ſecurity,
And feaſt my fill;—what could I wiſh for more?
Fool that I was, thus to be captive made!
I tremble at the doom that waits me now;
Yet whom have I to blame or to upbraid?
Myſelf alone; and to my fate I bow,
Convinc'd too late, that he is caught at laſt,
Who runs about too much and lives too faſt.

IMDERBIS juvenis, tandem cuſtode remoto;
　　Gaudet equis, canibuſque, et apricī gramine campi,
Cereus in vitium flecti, monitoribus aſper,
Utilium tardus proviſor, prodigus aeris,
Sublimis, cupiduſque, et amata relinquere pernix.

MINIMUM debet libere, cui nimium licet.—PLUTARCH. de Educat. lib. in fin.

Who moſt would act according to his will,
Requires moſt to be reſtrain'd from ill.

Fit ſpolians ſpolium.

The Spoiler is made Spoil.

ONE ſummer eve, beneath the greenwood ſhade,
　　I found young Phillis ſitting faſt aſleep.
With noiseleſs ſtep before th' unconſcious maid,
Joying to catch her in that ſlumber deep,
I ſtood and gaz'd; as though to feaſt my ſight
On ev'ry feature of her charming face:
And though her eye-lids veil'd from me their light,
Her rosy mouth, with such bewitching grace,
Seem'd as it were to proffer me the kiſs
So oft denied me with a ſmart rebuke;

That turning Thief at once, I stole the bliss;
But in that theft, lost more than what I took.
So, gentle reader, in the Love-chase too,
As with the mouse entrapp'd for love of bacon;
We're often made our very luck to rue,
Just when the thing most wished for has been taken.
I stole from her a kiss, but Phillis, she
At once stole heart and peace of mind from me;
The mouse, poor thing, lost life with liberty;
But without Phillis, what were life to me?
Oh! Love, thy pow'r surpasses all belief--
That Phillis sleeping, thus should steal the Thief!

Who poaching goes on Love's domain,
Oft loses where he thought to gain:
And when least thinking such may be,
To his surprise doth oft-times see,
Just like the mouse above pourtray'd,
Himself ensnar'd, and captive made.

—— Carpitque et carpitur unâ,
Suppliciumque suî est.—OVID.

Pœna comes Sceleris.

Punishment is the companion of Crime.

JUST as the greedy rat has seiz'd the bacon,
Down falls the trap, and lo! the thief is taken.
The prey though seized, of what avail to him?
That blow struck terror into every limb!
'Tis not enough to say: the evil deed
Brings its requital as the doer's meed:
The culprit from the moment of his crime,
Stung by his conscience through each hour of time,
Though none pursue, in each a captor sees,
Starts at each sound that's borne upon the breeze,
And where none other aught of terror deems,
Quails 'fore the hangman of his nightly dreams.

THE wicked flee when no man pursueth.— *Prov.* xxviii. 1.

OH coward conscience, how dost thou afflict me!
Cold fearful drops stand on my trembling flesh--
What do I fear?—Myself?—SHAKESPEARE.

WHICH way I move is Hell; myself am hell.—MILTON.

EVERY SIN CARRIES ITS OWN PUNISHMENT.

WHEN as the conqu'ring fleete return'd from Troy,
    And Pallas stormy wrath did them annoy;
Then Nauplius sought revenge upon the Greekes,
And hang'd out Lanterns on the rocky creekes;
The Greekes deceived did the rockes miftake,
And dashing gainst them did nights shipwracke make.

    Whilst we unto our wisht-for Country goe,
    This lifes fierce billowes tosse us to and fro;
    Honour and glory hang out lights fo faire,
    And Siren-like doe seeke us to ensnare:
    A joyfull, quiet haven they doe pretend;
    But oft they drave us to a dolefull end:
    If thou be wife shunne honours lights fo hy,
    And from shipwracking Siren pleasure fly.

FARLIE's *Emblems.*

A Barbe de Fol apprent à raire.

WILT GY SCHEREN NA DEN AERT?

BOO SCHEER VOOREERST EEN GECK SIJN BAERT.

WHO WOULD LEARN TO SHAVE WELL, SHOULD FIRST PRACTISE ON A FOOL'S BEARD.

THE Proverb is of antient date,
  That he who well would learn to ſhave,
His fulleſt wiſh to conſummate,
  Should on a Fool's beard practice have.
As with each phraſe of antient lore,
  The ſenſe implied hath ta'en its riſe

HE IS NA THE FOOL THAT THE FOOL IS,

From long experience gone before,
  That Fools to deal with maketh wife.
For Fools, of all men moſt precife
  In things of import leaſt, e'er gave
The wideſt fcope for practice nice
  Of Patience and of Virtues grave.
In ſhaving Fools the barber'll find
  Thofe Virtues to the utmoſt tried,
And howfoe'er to pleafe inclined,
  Both ſkill and patience mifapplied.
Of head and beard each fep'rate hair
  Muſt have the fame attention paid,
Muſt be arranged with niceſt care,
  And juſt as Fool will have it laid:
At ev'ry clip he fays, "Take heed!"
  And in the looking-glaſs muſt view
If all is done as he decreed,
  And what the Barber next muſt do:
This lock is now fomewhat too long,
  And this too ſhort—now here, now there,
There fomething ails, a curl lies wrong
  In beard or whiſker, or fomewhere.
On this fide now there needs anew
  Juſt—juſt a leetle ſnipp'd away,—
"So! let me look! yes! that will do—
  But here! this turn!—looks well? nay! nay!
No mouſtache ever look'd well fo,
  Like that indeed it cannot ſtay!"
And all the Barber ſtrives to do
  Is vain as all he tries to fay:
Yet! juſt this place behind the ear?
Aye! Fool! that's juſt the place that ail'd thee!
  From what we've feen 'tis very clear
It was the brains from firſt that failed thee!
  Who wants now this, now that, nor knows
What 'tis he needs, doth clearly ſhow it:
  For lacking brains, he feels and ſhows
He wants within the means to know it.

THERE IS NO CONCLUSION.

156

BY moryelicke beeren
Is veel te leeren.

'T moet een wijse hant sijn, die een sotten Kop wel scheren sal.
It must be a wise hand to cut the hair of a Fool's head.

WAT let, dat leert.
Quæ nocent, docent.

Παθήματα, μαθήματα.

VEXATIO dat intellectum.

HOMINE imperito nil quidquàm est injustius, qui, nisi quod ipse fecit nihil rectum
putat.—TERENT. *Adelph.*

MEN heeft groote kunst van doen
Om de narren te voldoen.

———

All those who appear Fools, are so, and no less, half of those who do not appear to be so.

FOLLY has a wide dominion in the World; and if there be some little Wisdom,
it is pure Folly compared with the Wisdom of the Most High. But the greatest
Fool is he, who does not believe that he is so, and who imputes Foolishness to every
body else. To be Wise, it is not sufficient to appear so to one's self. He is Wisest
who does not think that he is Wise; and he who does not perceive that others are,
does not see himself. How full soever the World be of Fools, there is no person who
thinks himself one, nor even, who suspects himself of folly.—GRACIAN.

THERE are People (in every class of Society) who entertain a high opinion of them-
selves, but those more particularly, who are the least worthy. Each considers himself
the centre of the Universe, and destined for an exalted position. Hope undertakes
rashly, and Experience renders it no assistance. Vain imagination finds an executioner
in Reality, who undeceives it. Every one should know his proper sphere of action,
and his fittest condition. Reality would then be the regulator of Self-Opinion.—*Idem.*

FORTUNE takes care that Fools should still be seen :
She places 'em aloft, o' th' topmost spoke
Of all her wheel. Fools are the daily work
Of nature, her Vocation : If she form
A Man, she loses by 't : 'tis too expensive ;
'T would make ten Fools : A Man's a Prodigy.

DRYDEN, *Œdip.*

UN Sot n'a pas assez d'étoffe pour être bon.—LA ROCHEFOUCAULD.

[left margin:] WIT IS FOLLY UNLESS A WISE MAN

[right margin:] HAS THE KEEPING OF IT.

MUCH like as wine the nurſe of Poets veine,
  When priſon-like the caſke doth it conteine;
Farre from the bottome while you draw the wine,
You will it find more plenteous and more fine;
But when you come to dreg, no wine abounds,
Both leaſt and worſt remaineth in the grounds:
Such like the ſhining of a candle we ſee,
Which kindled once burnes not ſtill equally;
At firſt it giv's greater and clearer light,
And is more pleaſant both to ſmell and ſight;
But when it comes to ſnuffe and even ſpent,
It ſhineth leſſe, and gives a filthy ſent.

  The candle and wine's our life, which, in its prime,
  Doth flouriſh more, and hath more hope of time;
  But when with muſtie age our life decayes,
  Then many ſorrowes have we, and few dayes.

FARLIE's *Emblems.*

HAS A FOOL FOR HIS MASTER.

ONE DOTH THE SCATH, ANOTHER HATH THE HARM.

Was de zeuge daet, moeten de biggen ontgelden.

MANY A ONE MUST PAY

FOR WHAT HE HAS NEVER ENJOYED.

WHAT THE SOW DOES, THE LITTLE PIGS MUST PAY FOR.

WHEN the old Sow has play'd her pranks,
    And upfet tubs and pails around her,
Out comes the Mafter in a rage,
    With broom in hand, refolv'd to pound her:

But fhe, well vers'd in all his oaths,
    And in their meaning full confiding,
Runs off and leaves her pigs behind
    To bear the blame and get the hiding.
And they, poor pigs, though innocent
    Of all the harm, defpite their fqueaking,
Get beat all round and made to fmart
    For all the big Sow has been breaking.

'Tis thus we often fee in life,
    The great mifdoers fave their bacon,
While blame and punifhment alike
    Fall on the fmaller folks when taken:
How Kings and Statefmen for their faults
    Get fcathelefs off, nor fear vexation,
While all the ills which they have wrought
    Are felt and paid for by the nation.

C E que la truye forfait, les porceaux souffrent.

QUIDQUID delirant Reges, plectuntur Achivi.—HORACE i. *Epift.* 2.

DAT veniam Corvis, vexat cenfura Columbas.—JUVEN. *Sat.* 2.

Πολλάκι καὶ ξύμπασα πόλις κακοῦ ἀνδρὸς ἐπαύρει.

Id eft,

SÆPE univerfa civitas viri mali scelera luit.

IL peccato del Signore souvente fa piangere il vassallo.
Un fa il peccato, l'altro la penitenza.

DER Herr sünd, der lauren büss.

WANNEER een Prins springt uyt den bant,
Daerom lijdt dickmael al het lant.

MANCHER muss entgelten des er nie genossen hat.

QUID agimus hoc cafu I feramus. Nam quemadmodum sterilitatem, aut nimios
imbres, aut cætera naturæ mala; ita luxum, ambitionem et avaritiam dominantium
habeamus.

THE DOVE HAS THE BLAME.

Sicilem rapuit, et agricola plectitur.—*Arabian Adage.* *Vid.* RICHT. *Axiom. Œcon.* 24, 25.

[*The same in another sense.*]

ITS GOOD FISHING IN TROUBLED WATERS.

The Reader will imagine a picture, representing a Fisher disturbing the water with a long pole, and driving the fish towards the net.

YOU wish to know what I'm about!
　　My bus'ness is soon told :
I'm going to fish upon a plan
　　Advis'd from time of old.
In waters that are most disturb'd,
　　Most fish are caught, they say ;
But when the water's calm and clear
　　The fish all swim away :
For then too cautiously they scan
　　The meshes of the net,
Or be your bait however good,
　　No bite from them you get.
But quite another sport it is
　　If you disturb the stream ;
The troubled water then gets thick,
　　And roach, perch, eels and bream
Are taken then alike at once,
　　Large fish as well as small,
All caught together in the net ;—
　　That's what I fishing call !

Need I say more! He who knows not
To make a stir in this World's stream,
Will but a sorry Fisher prove,
Nor minnows catch, much less a bream.
Stir, Fisher, stir! Stillness does harm ;
It little profits when the water's calm.

- ET multis utile bellum.—LUCAN. l. v. 182.

OPPORTUNI magnis conatibus transitus rerum.—TACITUS.

MULTI honores quos quietâ republicâ desperant, perturbatâ se consequi posse arbitrantur.—LIVY.

FAU trouble gain de pêcheur.

I CARRY about with me, my frugall ſtore,
  With which I am content, and ſeeke no more;
If it be meane, I can with it agree,
What ſtate ſoever, welcome comes to me:
I never begge, alive, what is diſtreſſe,
I know not; but once dead, I care for 't leſſe.
    Some live on others trenchers, and doe eate
    The bread of ſloth, for which they never ſweat:
    They're greedy ravens of mankind, kitching drones,
    Rich tables harpyes, rats, Chamelions.
    The wiſeman howſoever he doth ſinde
    Fortune, to it he ſits and frames his mind,
    He doth proferre his courſe and country faire,
    Unto his Patrons dole and diſhes rare.

FARLIE's Emblems.

Een Schip op een Zand, een Baken in Zee.

A SHIP AGROUND IS A BEACON AT SEA.

PORT! hard a-port! ftarboard your helm! look out!
　　See what our neighbour in the Schuyt's about!
Upon a fand-fpit there as fure as day,
He's hard and faft; right in the courfe we lay!
Give her a good wide berth, my mate, that we
Clear well the fand-tail where thofe breakers be.
They'll never poke her off—to ftrive is vain;
With ebbing-tide as now, there fhe'll remain:

And ſhould the wind chop round and blow to ſhore,
She'll break her rudder, or get damage more.
Reader! look well to this, and let it be
A caution in Life's voyage unto thee.
The Skipper who deſcries a ſhip aground,
No beacon needs to guide, nor lead to ſound:
And truly prudent is that man alone,
Who by another's fault can mend his own.

Many who have themſelves but little ſkill
　　To ſhape their courſe where peril may accrue,
Avert full oft the greater ſhare of ill,
　　Who take example from what others do.
For Youth, than this, there is no better ſchool
For Men, no milder diſcipline and rule,
Than well t' obſerve, and weigh with prudent care
The acts of others from the fruit they bear.

Ex vitio alterius Sapiens emendat ſuum.—P. Syrus.

Felix quem faciunt aliena pericula cautum.

Homines amplius oculis quam auribus credunt.—Seneca.

Longum iter est per præcepta, breve et efficax per exempla.—Ibid.

We do not want precepts, but patterns, for example is the gentleſt and least invidious way of commanding.—Pliny.

Example is a living rule that teaches without trouble to the learner, and lets him ſee his faults without open reproof and upbraiding.—Seaj. Palmer's *Aphoriſms*.

Example works more than precept; for words without practice are but counſels without effect.—*Ibid*.

I have given you an example, that ye ſhould do as I have done to you.—*John* xiii. 15.

Christ suffered for us, leaving us an example that we ſhould follow his ſteps.—1 *Pet.* ii. 21.

Chi ha mal vicin, ha mal matin.

'TIS well that ev'ry one should know
    Something of his next door neighbour;
What are his hours of to and fro!—
    Habits of life, and trade or labour?

For, whate'er our love of quiet,
    And our care to keep aloof,
If he's giv'n to drink and riot,
    Mischief soon may reach our roof.

Peaceful neighbours are a treasure
    To be wish'd for in this life;
But distressing beyond measure,
    Neighbours prone to noise and strife:

    All such people much require
    Watch and ward on all they do;
    Lest if their house should take fire,
    It perchance may spread to you.

Tunc tua res agitur paries cùm proximus ardet.—HORACE. i. *Epist.* 18.

Ne mala vicini pecoris contagia lædant.—VIRGIL, *Ecl.* 1.

Hinc benè commendavit Philosophus domum à bonis vicinis,
Aliquid mali propter vicinum malum.—PLAUTUS, *Mer.*

Mieux vaut être seul, que mal accompagné.
Beter alleen, als qualick verselt.

Of bad neighbours have a care.
Quade gebueren moet men berueren.

    Die ontrent den molen woont,
    Bestuyft het meel.

Zwischen Nachbarn Garten ist ein Zaun gut.

    Quando egli arde in vicinanza,
    Porta l'acqua à casa tua.

In the house of the righteous is much treasure: but in the revenues of the wicked is trouble.—*Proverbs* xv. 6.

IT IS GOOD TO HAVE A HEDGE.

LIGHTS ſtarre-like ſplendor doth allure this flye,
 Not knowing that ſhe may be burnt thereby:
Thus whilſt ſhe kindled with a great deſire
Of Light, loe now ſhee dies in flaming fire.

    Glory in purple robes is ſet on hie,
    Envious to many, lovely to the eye:
    But many times glory doth fooles undoe,
    Whilſt, without wit and reaſon, they it wooe:
    It raiſeth them that with the greater fall,
    It may them overthrow and cruſh withall.
    Whilſt Icarus ſoares to Hyperions beames,
    He headlong fals into th' Icarian ſtreames;
    And Pha'ton daring for to rule the day,
    Was thunder-beate, and burnt with Phœbus ray.

        We nearer to the Sunne more glorious are,
        If of the ſcorching rayes we be aware.

                    FARLIE's *Emblems.*

CHI DORME CO' CANI SE LIEVA CON PULCI.

HE THAT LIES DOWN WITH DOGS GETS UP WITH FLEAS.

E MEGLIO LASCIARE CHE MANCARE.

De gans blaest wel, maer en bjit niet.

GREAT BARKERS ARE NAE BITERS.

GREAT BOAST, SMALL ROAST.

THE GOOSE HISSES WELL, BUT IT DON'T BITE.

W HEN firſt theſe Geeſe I ſaw, and heard
    Them hiſs ſo ſierce at me ;
With fear o'erwhelm'd, I fled the bird,
    And thought therein to ſee
Some winged beaſt, or dragon ſell,
    Whoſe peſtilential breath

WORDS ARE BUT WIND, BUT BLOWS UNKIND.

Alone fufficed, as I'd heard tell,
　To fpread difmay and death.
At length their frappifh noife defpite,
　I felt within my breaft
A ftrange refolve to ftay my flight,
　And meet them at my beft.
So looking round as fiercely too,
　I was about to draw,
And pierce the hiffing monfters through;
　When all at once I faw—
And faid, as plain as I could fpeak:
　Why I'm a fool outright!
The beaft's a flat and toothlefs beak!
　With that he cannot bite;
No claws upon his feet has he
　That I had need to fear,
No crooked talons that I fee
　With which my flefh to tear.
'Tis all mere empty wind, e'en though
　So dread to th' ear and fight;
Fear not, my mates!—who hifs and blow
　Are feldom fierce to bite.

W IJT gapen, en bijt niet:
　　Veel blaaen en mijt niet.

Sv en bijten niet al, die haer tanden laten sien.

Chat mioleur ne fut jamais bon chasseur, non plus qu'homme sage caquetteur.

Een Kat die veel maeuwt, vangt weinigh muisen.

A much parola, obra poca
Can ch' abbaja, non vuol nocer.

Hühner die viel schwatzen, legen wenig Eier.
　Dov' è manca cor, quivi è piu lingua.

De grands vanteurs
Petits faiseurs.

Wenn die Worte Leute schlugen, so wär er ein tapferer Mann.

WORDS ARE GOOD WHEN WORKS FOLLOW.

Vasa inania plurimum tinniunt.

———An tibi Mavors
Ventosâ in linguâ, pedibusque fugacibus istis,
Semper erit!—Virg. Æn. ii.

Jam senectus mundi est, quæ est garrula.

Magis metuendi tacíturni et leves, quàm feroces et clamatores.

———Vana est sine viribus ira.

Minarum strepitus,
Asinorum crepitus.

Validior vox operis, quàm oris.

Ignavissimus quisque et in periculo minimum susurus nimù verbis, linguâ ferocet.
TACITUS.

Ut quisque ignavus animo, procax ore.—Ibid.

Quid dignum tanto feret hic promissor hiatu?
Parturiunt montes, nascetur ridiculus mus.—Horace.

Mons parturibat gemitus immanes ciens,
Eratque in terris maxima exspectatio.
At ille murem peperit. Hoc scriptum est tibi,
Qui magna cum minaris, extricas nihil.
Phædrus, Fabul. lxxix.

Canis timidus vehementiùs latrat, quàm mordet.—Curtius.

———Quid verbis opus est? spectemur agendo.—Ovid. xiii. Metam.

Multa verba, modica fides.—Richter, Axiom. Econ. iii.

Die Kühe die sehr brüllen, geben wenig Milch.
Hunde die sehr bellen, beissen nicht.

T is een wijse van het lant.
Lange tonge kort van hant.

Tel menace, qui est battu.
Tel menace, qui a grand' peur.
De grand menaceur peu de fait.

———Who knows himself a braggart
Let him fear this; for it shall come to pass
That every braggart shall be found an ass.
Shakespeare, All's Well that Ends Well.

Braggarts must needs be factious, for all bravery stands upon comparisons.
They must be violent to make good their vaunts. Neither can they be secret, and
therefore not effectual.—Lord Bacon.

WHEN as the waxen light and candle did fhine,
   As was the taper, fo the candle was fine:
When light is gone, this gives an odious fnuffe,
That fmels of Hyblas fweete nectarian ftuffe.
  So when the wicked fits in honours chaire,
  Unto the good man all doe him compare;
  But when Death fparing none, his mafke puls off,
  And changing Fortune fets him for a fcoffe:
  Then to the fritle people he doth flinke,
  His name fmels like a common-fhore or finke:
  The good againe, even in adverfiry,
  Cares not for Fortunes falfe inconftancy;
  And when againft him death hath done her beft,
  His name fmels like the Phenix fpicy neft.

                 FARLIE'S *Emblems.*

BETTER TRUST AN UNBRIDLED HORSE

THAN AN UNBRIDLED TONGUE.

Met onwillige honden is't quaet ha4en vangen.

WITH UNWILLING HOUNDS IT'S HARD TO CATCH HARES.

NOT far from here there lives a Maid,
   Who, as I've heard by many faid,
Will bring a good dow'r of gold and land
To him on whom fhe beftows her hand.
  A buxom, cheerful, buftling lafs,
  She leads her father's kine to grafs,

NO STRIVING AGAINST THE STREAM.

She bakes and she brews, she spins and sews,
And all a good housewife's duty knows.
 Nimble and neat of limb is she,
  Good temper'd too as a lass can be;
With pouting lips, and a cheek that glows
With all the hues of the opening rose:
 No burgher maid in Leyden town
 Can match her eyes of lustrous brown;
And were I now in my youthful prime,
To woo and win her I'd lose no time.

 I wish our Claes, that son of mine,
 Would but to my advice incline,
And court her close like a sensible lad,
While she and her dow'r may yet be had:
 For oft I've heard her father say:
 Whoe'er she choose, he'll not say nay;
But give her a well stock'd farm and land,
And a well fill'd purse besides in hand.

 But my son Claes, he is so slow,
 To her he will not courting go:
He only fancies the town-bred grace
Of a Courtly dame, and painted face.
 Yet what's your Court or burgher dame,
 With pride of birth and empty name.
To village lass with a purse well lin'd,
And wholesome both in body and mind?

 But, oh! this boy! 'tis vexing quite
 At hait so fair he will not bite;
And all I can do, or think, or say,
Alike on the lad are thrown away.
 How oft have I not brought him to
 The lass, in hopes that he would woo:
But there he'd stand—like a tongue-tied lout!
Nor open his mouth—but stare about!

 In vain to cheer him on I strive,
 And wink to make him more alive;
But not e'en once will he take her hand,
Nor speak one word she can understand.
 E'en though 'tis Fair-time now, yet he
 Buys her no Cakes nor Christmas tree;
No girdle, nor ring, nor handsome coif
To set the young damsel's head-dress off.

He writes no Sonnets in her praise,
 As is the custom now-a-days,
But cold as a stone, no word will say,
That hints at all at a Wedding-day.
 But, setting all such gifts aside—
 Though gifts are proper to a Bride—
Even from her he'll not take a thing,
Neither new neck-ruff, nor handsome ring!

WHO SO BLIND AS HE THAT WILL NOT SEE?

Yet lovers mostly have the sense
To look on gifts as no offence;
And if a young man will aught receive,
'Tis a sign—at least, so girls believe—
That he next day may come again,
And then p'rhaps speak his mind more plain;
For Love doth ever more hopeful burn,
When the receiver doth make return.
But oh! this Claes! he will not woo
As all as other people do!
E'en when she herself asks him to dance,
He says that he can't, and looks askance!
For her he has no pleasing talk;
He never takes her out to walk,—
And when she kindly asks him to stay,
He takes up his hat to walk away!—
To lose such a chance to me is odd!—
Now isn't my Claes a downright clod!

But now I find my wife was right,
When she said to me t'other night:
Do hold thy tongue, now, Father, do!
'Tis plain our Claes don't care to woo.
Thou'lt never bring the match to pass,
He has no taking to the lass:
He's p'rhaps some other girl in view,
And take my word you may for true;—
The Love that's forced will never do!
Is not a lover, after all,
Best judge on whom his choice should fall!
Is courting not an impulse free,
That knows no force nor law's decree!
Do, Father, let the boy alone;—
Compulsion never yet was known
To rule th' affections of the heart,
Nor guide the course of Cupid's dart.
Let him be free to choose his mate
According to his heart's dictate:
"No Well so bad as that, we think,
Whose water we're compelled to drink."
Is not the Love-chase just the same
As hunting any other game!
What though the sportsman even see
The hare, so tame as not to flee,
Squat here and there at distance short,
As though the very dogs to court;—
Yet none the more the hare is won
If that his dogs refuse to run:
For hounds which hunt against their will,
Were seldom known the game to kill.

I AM confumed with devouring fire,
  Whilft Vulcane gainft me doubles thus his ire:
The hand, much like an Ifthme, doth feparate
The flames, and doth it felfe præcipitate
Into open danger, fhewing fo its love,
The fcorching flames compels it to remove.
    A thriftleffe hufband if he fpend his ftate,
    And fo the wife loving to gœ too neat;
    Their ftocke and meanes quickely goes to decay,
    And late repentance comes, when all's away.
    But if a friend their ruine would prevent,
    And ftay their fall; be fure he fhall be fhent:
    He lofing labour fcarce fhall harmleffe gœ,
    They both againft him turne their malice fo.
    Oft times who parteth quarrels and debate,
    Againft himfelfe doth turne the parties hate.
                        FARLIE'S *Emblems.*

THE LABOUR WE DELIGHT IN PHYSICS PAIN.

THERE BELONGS MORE THAN WHISTLING TO GOING TO PLOUGH.

Om wijnigh Graens een gansche Moole.

Text along left side of image: GREAT DOINGS AT GREGORY'S

Text along right side of image: HEAT THE OVEN TWICE FOR A CUSTARD.

A WHOLE MILL TO GRIND A PECK OF CORN.

EH! Mafter, what is all this work,
 This hamm'ring, fawing, clatter?
Each morning that I wake of late
 I wonder what's the matter!
What is't that you are building here?
 A mill, forfooth! but furely
So large a Mill as this will be
 A lofs of money purely;

For in this fack of yours I feel
    So little corn for grinding,
That when you've made it into meal
    'Twill fcarce be worth your minding.
A Hand-mill would be large enough
    To grind this corn, good neighbour!
And if you'd be advifed by me
    You'd ceafe your ufelefs labour.
You may rely, this Mill of yours
    Will yield you little profit,
'Twill foon ftand ftill, or, what is worfe,
    You'll be obliged to let it:
Don't fpend your money thus, my friend,
    'Tis hard enough to find it;
Who only hath a peck of corn
    Need build no Mill to grind it.

TRUDITUR dies die,
    Novæque pergunt interire lunæ.
Tu fecanda marmora
    Locas fub ipfum funus, et fepulcri
Immemor ftruis domos.—HORAT. li. Od. 18.

Senes, inquit Arnisæus, spolia opima marinæ Deæ suspendere debent, cum hac inscriptione.—(De Jur. Connub.)

Vixi puellis nuper idoneus,
Et militavi non fine gloria,
Nunc arma defunctumque bello
Hunc gladium paries habebit.
            HORAT. lib. Od. 26.

——Define dulcium
Mater fæva Cupidinum.—Idem lv. Od. 1.

Circa horam decem flectere mollibus
Jam durum imperiis : abi
Quò blandæ juvenum te revocant preces.

Een oudt man met een jonge vrou,
Wat kan het wesen als berou !

C'est chose aussi follastre de voir le gendarme qui va au baston, que l'amoureux qui ne peut marcher sans aide.

Veel geschreeus en luttel wolle.
Veel vlagen luttel boter.

La più guasta rota del carro
Fa sempre maggior strepito.
Viel geschrey, wenig wollen.
Grosse word und nichts da hinder.

— · —

Ne'er put the Plough afore the Oxen.

In every undertaking, that which is Essential should have the first place ; and the Accessory, if there is occasion for it, should be considered afterwards. Many men commence with that which is of least moment to them, and defer the consideration of those things which would be useful and profitable, to a period when it is too late to reap the advantages which would accrue from them. We thus frequently see men who have no sooner begun to prosper in life, than they become eclipsed as it were in their very success, and emerge in poverty. Method is as necessary to the art to live, as to the acquirement of Knowledge.

Selon le pain il faut le couteau.
Selon ta bourse gouverne ta bouche.
Fou est qui plus dépense que sa rente ne vaut.

Stretch out your legs according to the length of your blanket.

One ounce of discretion is worth a pound of wit.

Chi tutto abbraccia, nulla stringa.

Ce qui vient au son de la flûte s'en va au son du tambour.

Make no more haste than good speed.

Cavendum est, ne in festinationibus suspicionibus nimias celeritates.—Cicero.

Qui unumquodque mature transegit, is properat ; qui multa simul incipit neque perficit, festinat.—Cato.

— — —

TITANS day burning lamp is fet on high,
    The more to light'n the Earth from faphir fky;
His beames more glorious and confpicuous fhine
From Eaſt to Weſt, from South to midnight line:
My light you muſt not under buſhell put,
Nor in a chinky corners prifon ſhut;
That lights may cleare the chambers all throughout,
They muſt aloſt be hanged round about.

    You holy Prieſts, to whom the word oſ light
    Is truſt, advance your torches in the ſight
    Of mortals, ſhew them who in darkeneſſe dwell,
    The narrow way that leads to Heaven, from Hell.

                              FARLIE's *Emblems.*

Two Dogges strive for a Bone, and the third taketh it away.

THE DOGS AND THE BONE.

ALL ye who would a Moral learn,
Your eyes upon this Emblem turn:
Two dogs in combat fierce you fee,
For Dogs, like Men, will difagree.
The caufe of quarrel was a bone,
With dogs a very frequent one;
But while the two in deadly fight,
Half blind with rage, bark, tear and bite,

More bent each other's flesh to wound
Than heed the bone upon the ground;
Up comes a third, attracted by
The brawl and, quick the cause t' espy,
Snaps up the bone without ado,
And with it disappears from view.
The combatants, whose kindled bile
Had somewhat settled down the while,
Exhausted almost with the fight,
At once both miss the bone from sight!
And quick as thought, with one consent,
They cease the fray, and both intent
To find the prize for which they fought,
With eager haste the bone is sought:
But all in vain, no bone is there,—
But foam and bloodstains everywhere,
Mingled with clotted flakes of hair.
At length away the dogs depart,
In pain and discontent of heart,
That they, who fought the prize to gain,
Should doubly losers thus remain;
While some one, who no risk had run,
The "bone of their contention" won.
Such things and like results are seen
T' occur full oft young folks between;
Among the People oft'ner still,
And Princes, where there's want of skill.

But while I'm on this subject now,
An instance I'll relate to you,
Of which I've known before to-day
Full many end the self-same way.
Two suitors woo'd a Burgher maid,
With dow'ry rich, and each afraid
His rival should with her prevail,
Bethought him all he could t' assail
And prejudice the other's name,
That he might best secure the game.

WHAT FORCE CANNOT DO, INGENUITY MAY.

With feelings such on either fide,
Throughout the City, far and wide,
Reports were current foon of each,
Which did fo mutually impeach
Their name and fame, that fwords alone
Could for fuch calumnies atone,
They met—they fought—the younger fell;
His rival's blade prov'd all too well
The bitter rancour of the thruft
That ftretch'd him proftrate in the duft.
Though victor, yet compell'd to fly,
T' efcape the Duel's penalty;
The field at once of both made clear,
Another fuitor now drew near;
Who, though before but little feen,
Had ne'er the lefs, like them too, been
A Fifher in the felf-fame ftream,
Though not prefuming fuch to feem;
And boldly now he fets his fail,
To profit by the fav'ring gale;
Declares in all its honeft truth
The love that had o'ercaft his youth;
Subdues at once the damfel's pride,
And changes Sweetheart into Bride.
The Brawlers, when they both return'd
To health and home, the tidings learn'd,
That one far more difcreet than they,
Advantage taking of their fray,
Had won the Prize the proper way.

DUMOS concussi, sustuli alter aves.
  Sic vos non vobis nidificatis aves.
  Sic vos non vobis vellera fertis oves.
  Sic vos non vobis mellificatis apes.
  Sic vos non vobis fertis aratra boves.

    Tel est les buissons
    Qui n'a pas les oisillons.

WHILST THE DOGS ARE GROWLING AT EACH OTHER,

YEE WOLF DEVOURS THE SHEEP.

WHAT e're my flat's my love proves conftant ftill,
　　To this my Soule, we part againft our will;
Or when fierce Boreas with his bluftring gale,
Or fome mifchance my lovely light doth quale:
Elfe I and Light my life, would never part,
Before to afhes fates did me convert.

　　Nature commands us to maintaine our breath
　　And being, fhunning life-deftroying death.
　　Yet man from Atropus oft takes the knife,
　　And cuts his fatall thred devouring life:
　　For why, he fearing death before his day,
　　Before th'allarum, makes himfelfe away.
　　Ah wretch I unworthy to behold the fkye,
　　Who will not live, and knowes not how to dye.
　　　　　　　　　　　　FARLIE'S *Emblems.*

Nemo potest Thetidem simul et Galatean amare.

NO ONE CAN LOVE THETIS AND GALATEA
AT THE SAME TIME.

LISTEN, Mates! attend to me,
   I would fomething to you fay,
That may of fome fervice be—
   Rather curious in its way!
I've a fondnefs for the Fair,
   Which, my reafon all defpite,
Makes me ev'ry day defpair
   Where to fix my heart aright.

GRASP ALL, LOSE ALL.

Ev'ry pretty girl I meet,
  Sets my heart in such a stir,
That, without the least deceit,
  I would make strong love to her.
Thus so wav'ring in my mind,
  Two girls now at once I woo;
But I've long begun to find
  'Tis much more than I can do.
One is Galatea nam'd,
  And the other, as you know,
Thetis—for her beauty fam'd,
  Spoken of where'er you go.
Thetis lives down by the Sea;
  Galatea on the Moor;
Thetis talks of ships to me,
  And of things along the shore.
Galatea, lively lass!
  Speaks of dairies, and of cows,
Of the meadows, and the grass,
  And the crops her father grows;
Of the tuneful woods and fields,
  Where the sheep in hundreds stray,
What their fleece in profit yields,
  And the joys of market-day:
Speaks of shady lanes to me,
  With their hedgerows green and gay,
And the Linden trees where we
  Often chat an hour away.
Thetis too tells pleasing tales
  In the Fishers' homely talk;
How in Greenland they catch whales,—
  Charming 'tis with her to walk!
Herring nets to make and mend
  Then she tells me how, and I
Long a helping hand to lend,
  When she spreads them out to dry.
Plaice and flounders how they take,—
  And how cure them on the shore;

How one man of fiſh may make
  Oft a catch of twenty ſcore:
How they fiſh with hook and net,
  All ſo pleaſing like and true,
That by her bright eyes of jet,
  I'm both hook'd and netted too.
Galatea ſays that ſhe
  Likes no fiſh, nor thoſe who live
Or by fiſhing, or the ſea,
  But the reaſon ſhe won't give.
Galatea's conſtant theme
  Is her butter and her cheeſe;—
" What's your *fiſh* compared to cream ?
  Soles or plaice (ſays ſhe) to theſe ! "
If I ſpeak of fields and trees,
  Or the leaſt of farm-things ſay,
Thetis' look's enough to freeze
  And ſhe takes her hand away :
If I wear a fiſher's dreſs,
  Galatea from me turns,
And, when in farm-clothes, no leſs,
  Thetis all my wooing ſpurns.
When my fiſher's cap I've on,
  Fluſhings looſe and jacket rough,
Galatea ſays, Begone !
  But her look is quite enough !
If in ſhepherd's ſlouch I go,
  Thetis, if ſhe chance to ſee,
Calls me Boor ! and jeers me ſo,
  That all eyes are turn'd on me !
Thus for two long years have I
  Chaſed this game, and nothing caught ;—
Just as one " who hunts two hares,
  Loſes both, and catches naught."
So, Mates, when you wooing go,
Fool is he who my way chooſes ;
Who at once courts ſweethearts two,
Pleaſes neither, and both loſes !

BEHOLD the Bridegroome comes, he takes his way,
  Nor Man, nor Angell knowes the houre or day;
He faies, he'le come, much like a theefe in night,
To judge the world with equity and right;
Angels fhall charge with trumpets founding cleare,
And Chrift as Judge fhall in the clouds appeare;
The righteous and the wicked fhall arife,
Bodies and Soules, to paffe upon that 'fize.
He who the oyle of preparation hath,
Whom Chrift fhall find furnish'd with faving faith;
Shall with the bleffed Bridegroome mount on hie,
Mongft Seraphimes triumphing glorioufly;
But he who hath no oyle, nor faith at all,
Heavens dreadfull Judge fhall that man curfed call,
And banifh him into the pit of hell,
Where with the fiends for ever he muft dwell.

FARLIE's Emblems.

In Recessu Nihil.

A FAIR FACE MAY HIDE A FOUL HEART.

A FAIR FACE MAY BE A FOUL BARGAIN.

WITHIN IS EMPTINESS.

YOU say that Isabella is of such surpassing grace,
   So beautiful in form, and ev'ry feature of her face;
   That you're surpris'd I do not ask her hand at once, as you
Affirm, if you were in my place, you would without ado.
But, Friend, you are mistaken, and you estimate too high
The beauty of a figure, and the lustre of an eye:
These I admit she has, but something still I wanting find—
Though beautiful in face,—she wants the beauty of the mind.

BELLE CAGE, SANS OISEAU.

She's like the handfome Monument, to which the fculptor's art
Has given grace and fymmetry to every outward part ;
Externally adorn'd with all that moft the eye can win,
All outward fhew like that is fhe, but empty all within.
Pay lefs regard to Form and Face, when you felect a wife ;
The Beauty of the Mind alone is that which lafts for life.

MISTAKEN Nature here has join'd
    A beauteous face and ugly mind ;
In vain the fau'tless features ftrike,
When soul and body are unlike :
Pity that snowy breast should hide
Deceit and avarice and pride.—Pope.

Nam divinitus interdum, Venerique sagittis,
Deteriore fit ut formâ muliercula ametur ;
Nam facit ipsa suis interdum femina factis,
Morigerisque modis, et mundo corpore culta,
Ut facile insuescat vir secum ducere vitam.—Lucret.

Plus aliquid formâ est, plus est oculisque genisque ;
Plus aliquid toto corpore, quidquid amo.—Dan. Heynsius.

Sit procul omne nefas, ut ameris amabilis esto ;
Quod tibi non facies, solaque forma dabit.—Ovid.

Temerariis judiciis plena sunt omnia, de quo desperamus subito convertitur, et fit
optimus ; de quo multum præsumpseramus, deficit et fit pessimus, nec timor noster
certus est, nec amor.—August. de Past.

Judge not according to the Appearance, but judge righteous judgment.
John vii. 24.

The Lord seeth not as man seeth ; for man looketh on the outward appearance,
but the Lord looketh on the heart.—1 *Sam.* xvi. 7.

Favour is deceitful, and Beauty is vain ; but a woman that feareth the Lord, she
shall be praised.—*Proverbs* xxxi. 30.

Tel semble sage en apparence,
Qui fol est en quintessence.

Fronti nulla Fides.

WHEN travellers first the Pyramids behold,
  Lifting their sun-lit tops in contrast bold
Against the splendour of th' Egyptian sky;
Their grand dimensions to the fancy brings
The semblance of the Palaces of Kings;
  So great is their external majesty !
But what are they within?—No Halls are there,
No Royal Courts, nor Princely Chambers fair,
  The imaged scenes of Eastern pageantry.
What then ! mere dust ! the Ashes of the Dead !
Around, within, on every side outspread
  In one drear, dread Sepulchral mockery !

'Tis thus we are instructed to beware
  Of judging from Appearances alone ;
"The Castles that we image in the air"
  Are not more empty—when the truth is known.

—

Plus en a de fonds, et plus en est homme.

THE inside ought always to be worth as much again as the outward appearance.
  There are people who have exterior only ; resembling houses which have not
been finished for want of funds ; the entry is palatial, the inside a hovel. This kind
of Persons presents nothing to fix the attention, or rather, all within them is fixed ;
for after the first salutation the conversation is ended. They make their introductory
bow, after the fashion of the Sicilian horses, which after one or two caracoles become
suddenly metamorphosed into motionless taciturnity. For words are soon exhausted
when the mind is barren. It is easy for them to deceive others who like themselves
have nothing but appearance, but they are objects of pity to persons of discernment,
who soon discover that they are empty within.—GRACIAN'S *Maxims.*

Tinnit ; inane est.

ITS empty : hark, it sounds : 'tis vain and void,
  What's here to be enjoy'd
But grief and sickness, and large bills of sorrow,
  Drawn now, and cross'd to-morrow !
Or what are men, but puffs of dying breath,
  Reviv'd with living death !
Fond youth, oh, build thy hopes on surer grounds
  Than what dull flesh propounds :
Trust not this hollow world, 'tis empty : hark, it sounds.
                                        QUARLES' *Emblems.*

W HO fo beholds this fmoaky fnuffe of mine,
He muft needs thinke that fometime I did fhine;
But now my Light is gone, my glory's darke,
Onely of light I have the brand and marke.
  Who for his Country hath with valour flood,
  His wounds doe fhew, that he hath fpent his blood:
  In Venus training who hath beene practifed,
  Some token he beares of what he exercifed.
  The Schollars badge, are fallow lookes and blanch,
  The gluttons is the fatneffe of his panch,
  Verrue and vice doth leave fome token behind,
  Which of themfelves doe put us ftill in minde.

FARLIE'S *Emblems*.

BE SLOW IN CHOOSING,

BUT SLOWER IN CHANGING.

Vechtende Koryen vergen haar te samen, als de Wolf komt.

SINGLY WE SUCCUMB,

UNITED WE CONQUER.

WHEN THE WOLF COMES, THE OXEN LEAVE OFF FIGHTING TO UNITE IN SELF-DEFENCE.

NOT long ago, fome oxen of our herds upon the moor,
   In furious fight among themfelves, as oft I've feen before,
   Were fuddenly furpris'd to fee fome Wolves, which, crouching low,
Were ftealing on the herd to ftrike an unexpected blow.
Like magic, all at once, th' inteftine feuds and bloodfhed ceafe,
As though the common danger had fubdued them all to peace:
And quick,—as if imprefs'd with all the folly of their ftrife;
Made fenfible that Union alone could fave the life

L'UNION FAIT LA FORCE.

Of each and all,—to face the foe they haste a ring to form,
And croup to croup clofe prefs'd make front to meet th' impending ftorm.*
'Twas juft in time! for fcarcely were they marfhall'd back to back,
When down upon the herd already burfts the rav'ning pack:
But all in vain the Wolves affail; for everywhere they meet
A phalanx of oppofing horns, their onfet fierce to greet;
And high in air uptofs'd, or difembowell'd on the plain,—
The few remaining take to flight, nor dare th' affault again.

So fhould confed'rate States and Peoples hufh all inward ftrife,
When from without a foreign foe affails the Nation's life;
All difcords then out-trodden—'tis by Unity alone
The Free fhall fave their Freedom, and the Brave preferve their own.

— — · —

CONCORDIA parvæ res crescunt : discordiâ autem maximæ dilabuntur.
SALLUST. *Jugurth.*

TWIST verquist.

EENDRAGT geeft magt
Eenigkeyt vermag veel.

VERDEELT vyer brandt qualick.
Scaner'd fire burns badly.

SACRUM est Pacis nomen, et quod vix terram sapiat : nec alio nomine Hebræi Tò εἰρήν, ipsam adeò perfectionem, innuebant : nec quid aliud humano generi lubentius vel gratulati sunt Angeli, vel legavit Christus, vel Apostoli præceperunt, &c.
JOSEPH HALL, *Rom. Irreconciliab.*

Kryg van buiten
Doet vrientschap sluiten.

COMMUNE periculum dissidentes conjungit. Instante communi periculo, conciliari solent dissidentium animi.—DIONYS. *Halicarn. lib.* 8.

— — —

* The instinctive resort of horned cattle to this mode of defence against the wolf, is more especially remarkable, and of very frequent occurrence, among the herds of half wild horses in the Bukowina, and on the Pusztas of Hungary, with the difference that these form the "Karika" or ring, with their heels outwards, in order to give the wolves the full advantage of that characteristic and efficient mode of defence of the horse.—*Note of Translator.*

Ne point montrer le doigt malade.
Shew not where your finger ails.

For every one will strike you there. Beware also to complain of it, for in as much as Malice always attacks the weakest point, the show of resentment and suffering only serves to gratify and to divert it. The malice of mankind always endeavours to unhinge; it gives utterance to cutting words, and resorts to every expedient, until it has discovered the sore, where it can pierce to the quick. The man of sense and tact never exposes his weak point, whether personal or hereditary; because Fortune herself takes delight sometimes in wounding the place where she knows the pain will be felt most acutely. She always mortifies to the quick. Consequently it is requisite to conceal from mankind all knowledge both of that which mortifies, and of that which gives satisfaction; in order to bring the former to the speediest termination, and to make the latter endure the longer.—GRACIAN.

Strength is increased by Concord.

The fast faggot is not easily broken.

L'Union fait la Force.

Auxilia humilia firma consensus facit.

Unius dissensione totus consensionis globus disjectus sit.—NEPOS.

Adversity tries friends.

In angustia amici boni apparent.

God helps those who help themselves.

Fortes Fortuna juvat.

Timidi nunquam statuere tropæum.—SUIDAS ex Euripide.

Il n'y a que les honteux qui perdent.

Audaces Fortuna juvat, timidosque repellit.

Qui ipsi sibi sapiens prodesse nequis, ne quidquam sapis.
CICERO, Ep. lib. vii.

In circumstances of difficulty, there is no better company than a resolute heart; and if that should happen to fail, it should be aided by the Mind. Difficulties grow less for them who know how to help themselves. Submit not to the strokes of adversity without an effort to overcome them, lest they become less endurable. Some persons help themselves so little in their troubles, that they increase them, for want of knowing how to meet and bear them with courage. He who knows himself well, finds assistance to his weakness in reflection. The man of judgment comes out of every dilemma with credit and advantage to himself.

WHILST I give light to others, I decay;
    I lofe my felfe, whilft I to others play:
I watch all night with an unfleepy eye,
And oft, before the day doth dawne, I dye:
How oft am I by bluftering Boreas mockt,
And lighting others, I my felfe am chokt;
If tumult, of a night affailing be,
I am employ'd, no reft, no peace for me:
What moft of men neglect, that I ohferve,
To fuccour others, though my felfe fhould ftarve:
A Law but not of nature, which directs
All of themfelves to have the prime refpects.
    Codrus the King, his Country to defend,
    Much like a Prodigall his life did fpend;
    The Pelican to fœde her plumeleffe brood,
    Doth lance her breaft, and ftraine her pureft blood,
    The watchfull fheepherd feldome feeing fleepe,
    Directs, and keepes from wolves his ftraying fheepe:
    Even Chrift himfelfe, the Sonne of the moft Hie,
    Did fuffer death, left mortall man fhould die.

FARLIE's Emblems.

BOLDNESS IS PRUDENCE.

WHILE YOU TRUST TO THE DOG,

THE WOLF SLIPS INTO THE SHEEP-FOLD.

Dum plorat, vorat.

FEMME RIT QUAND ELLE PEUT,

ET PLEURE QUAND ELLE VEUT.

WHILE SHE WEEPS, SHE DEVOURS.

CALLING a few days since to pay
  A vifit to my fweetheart fair,
Her face quite fill'd me with difmay,
  She look'd fo pale and wan with care.
That fhe, fo full of life and fong,
  As was her wont, thus fad fhould be,
Made me conclude, that fomething wrong
  Had her befall'n—or p'rhaps that fhe
  Had got fome filly doubts of me.

VRIENT, LET'ER OP, MEN VINT'ER NOCH.

Well, dearest love!—but what is this?
  What ails? what has occurr'd to thee?
Why then so cold?—not e'en one kiss!—
  Art ill—or discontent with me?
Nay, nay, thou'rt ill I'm sure—I see,
  I know it by thy drooping eye,
Thou lookst not as thou'rt wont on me,
  Come let me know,—why then that sigh?—
  Speak, speak, did I yet aught deny?

But long she made me no reply,
  Though still she sigh'd, and I could see,
The more I said, the more her eye
  Was fill'd with tears, and turn'd from me;
Until at length quite griev'd, I said,
  Come cease this weeping—speak then, th—
Tell me thy grief, nor be afraid;
  If silent thus, how can I know
  In what to aid or comfort you?

On this upon my arm she laid
  Her pretty hand, and murm'ring low—
Alas! 'tis this—(the sighing said)
  My cause of grief, since you will know :
A sad misfortune I have had!
  That e'er so luckless I could be!
I've lost—I'm sure I shall go mad—
  That handsome ring you gave to me!
  Which all admir'd who us'd to see.

And then—Oh! woe is me!—to-day,
  While walking in the Park, I felt
The Bracelet on my arm give way,—
  I really thought my heart would melt:
I look'd, and lo! the diamond clasp
  Which held the string of pearls I wear,
Had broken somehow at the hasp!—
  You know what splendid pearls they were?
  Well! eight are lost, I do declare!

Oh! how shall I this loss repair!
  All thy best presents thus to lose ;—
I've scarce a jewel now to wear!!
  And fifty pounds won't replace those!

When she had ended this lament,
Her sobs and tears came fast anew,
And I, upon her grief intent,
Knew neither what to say or do,
And truth to say, 'twas vexing too.

When just as I was deep in thought,
How best her grief somewhat t' allay,
A Jeweller my notice caught,
Who seem'd by chance t' have come that way.
Greeting us both with much respect,
He op'd his caskets to our view:
And said—Sir, p'rhaps you'll not object
To let me shew some rings to you—
And to my lady, something new?

She, (so it seem'd) her grief appeas'd
At once, at sight of all his ware,
A costly diamond ring first seis'd,
The finest, largest he had there;
And said :—Ah! this is just the kind
Of ring that I have wish'd for so!
Had I but now a generous friend
To buy me that!—'twould soothe my woe!
And, as she spoke, she kiss'd me too.

I, mov'd to see her mournful face,
Ask'd him the cost; and being told,
Began to bid for it apace;
I found I'd just the sum in gold:
But nothing in the price would he
Abate—and she, with eyes still red,
Look'd in my face so anxiously !—
That e'er I well knew what I said,
The ring was bought, and money paid.

That I'd been cheated to my face,
Since then I found to my surprise!
The thing was plann'd to time and place,
It was her Brother in disguise!
'Twas her own diamond ring that I
Had bought and paid for o'er anew!
So when you see your Sweetheart cry,
Take heed, my Friends, what 'tis you do.
But laugh or weep 'tis much the same,
They're both the sex's Winning Game.

WHEN that my clammy fubflance was entire,
　　I was an earthly nurfe of heav'n-bred fire;
Now envious time doth me in afhes turne,
And to a tedious fnuffe my light doth burne:
Loe I have done, take thou this light of mine;
I yeeld, doe what thou canft, the turne is thine.
So the Comedian having plaid his fhare,
Gives place to others, who then actors are:
A King his weighty office having done,
Dying tranffers his Scepter to his fonne:
When that the crafie Souldiers ftrength doth faile,
The younger muft the enemy affaile.
　　Happy is he the evening of whofe daies
　　Doth crowne his death with ever-living bayes.

FARLIE'S *Emblems*.

A FOOLISH WOMAN IS CLAMOROUS.

Cedendo Victor abibis.

YIELDING IS SOMETIMES THE BEST WAY OF SUCCEEDING.

OAKS MAY FALL WHEN REEDS BRAVE THE STORM.

BY YIELDING THOU MAY'ST CONQUER.

THAT the flender Reed you fee,
    Chaf'd and driven by the blaft,
Should not foon uprooted be,
    Or upon the waters caft ;—
That fo frail a thing in form
    Is not quickly borne away,
Rent to tatters by the ftorm,
    Is a wondrous thing, you fay ?

FLECTI NON FRANGI.

Since so oft the stately Oak,
  Tow'ring upward to the skies,
Is uprooted by the stroke,
  E'en despite its strength and size!
Strange as this may seem to thee,
  'Tis with wise instruction rife,
And imports how men may be
  Victors in the storms of Life.
Things of lowly growth and height
  Have but little weight to bear;
And, whate'er the tempest's might,
  Feel it in diminish'd share:
Less expos'd to every wind
  Than the lofty forest trees,
Humbler plants a quiet find
  That is seldom known to these.
Fragile though the Reed appear
  To resist so fierce a blast,
Yet it hath no need to fear;
  For when once the gale is past,
Lifting then its head anew,
  Still unharm'd, o'er fen and lake,
Proves the antient maxim true,
  " That which bends, doth seldom break. "

AUREAM quisquis mediocritatem
    Diligit, tutus caret obsoleti
Sordibus tecti, caret invidendâ
        Sobrius aulâ.
                        HORACE, lib. ii. Od. 10.

  Felix, mediæ quisquis turbæ
  Parte quietus, aurâ stringit
  Littora tuta, timidusque mari
  Credere cymbam, remo terras
  Propriore legit.—SENECA, Agamem.

CREDE mihi, benè qui latuit, benè vixit, et intrâ
  Fortunam debet quisque manere suam.—OVID.

Rebus in adversis facile est contemnere vitam,
 Fortiter ille facit qui miser esse potest.

In adverse times, 'tis easy of life's burdens to complain;
But nobler far, with fortitude to suffer, and sustain.

The gods take pleasure oft when haughty mortals
On their own Pride erect a mighty fabric,
By slightest means to lay their towering schemes
Low in the dust, and teach them they are nothing.
                                        THOMSON.

Though plung'd in ills, and exercis'd in care,
Yet never let the noble mind despair:
When press'd by dangers, and beset by foes,
The gods their timely succour interpose;
And when our Virtue sinks, o'erwhelm'd with grief,
By unforeseen expedients bring relief.—PHILIPS.

Storms often fell the stately oak,
High mountains feel the thunder's stroke;
And lofty tow'rs, when winds assail,
In their resistance less prevail
Than doth the reed upon the shore,
Which rises when the storm is o'er.

Confido, conquiesco.

O!! Source of every good, and every joy,
 Meek resignation felt without alloy;
Jehovah! from whose ever bounteous store,
Mercy, and joy, untainted blessings pour;
Who bids us ask, and asking not amiss,
Convey'st an heavenly, in an earthly bliss;
Whose hand protects us, and whose eye pervades,
Whose promise cheers us, and whose grace persuades:
Though thron'd on high, where blessed spirits bow,
And blissful minds sublimest raptures know;
Yet stooping low as earth, our prayers are heard,
Our wants reliev'd, and all our sorrows cheer'd:
Alike thy fondness to thy creatures shew'd
In what's withholden as in what's bestow'd.
Then let me pause—and if presumptuous thought
My humble state bewails, or grieves at aught;
O soothe with calm content, that I may share
Thy gifts with grateful heart, whate'er they are.—Anon.

IF thus my light nights fable filence glads,
  Making a cheerefull roome in midnight fhads;
If Gold'n-like Phœbus and his filver fifter,
He in the day, fhee in the night doth glifter;
What thought-furpaffing light then fhall that be,
When we in Heaven Empyrean God fhall fee?
Sooner thou canft the world hold in thy hand,
Or in a fhell containe the glaffie ftrand;
Than tell how glorious is the light of Heaven,
That dark'ns the Sunne, Moone, Stars, and Planets feven:
This onely tell: it is not Phœbus light,
Nor Phœbus, nor the fpangles of the night.
That light which tongue cannot, nor mind defcry,
Once fhalt thou fee, a fupreame Deity.

FARLIE's Emblems.

PARVIS COMPONERE MAGNA

COMPARE SMALL WITH GREAT

HIGH HOUSES ARE MOSTLY EMPTY IN THE UPPER STORY.

HIGH TREES GIVE MORE SHADOW THAN FRUIT.

Assài rumori, e poco lana.

GREAT CRY AND LITTLE WOOL.

HEREIN we see a somewhat novel Sight,
 To which the Reader's notice we invite:
One man doth shear a Sheep, and strange to see,
Another shears a Pig in company.
Let us consider what this thing may mean;
Perchance therefrom some lesson we may glean.
He, who the Pig doth shear, the senseless lout,
Believes he knows full well what he's about;

VEEL GESCHREEUWS, EN LUTTEL WOL.

And that when done, to him there will accrue
By far the greater profit of the two.
The Pig's the heaviest beast he thinks, no doubt,
Has thickest fat, and much the longest snout;
But the unruly brute, like all his kind,
Is hard to manage, nor at all inclin'd
To yield submissive to his treatment new,
And gives his Shearer roughish work to do.
Rending the air with shrillest, piercing shrieks,
He kicks and struggles, twists about and squeaks
With such untiring strength and energy,
That all the neighbours round look out to see,
Or gather near to ascertain aright
The real meaning of so strange a sight.
Amid much trouble, and the jeers of all,
He shortly finds his profit very small,
For in the place of Wool, what is't he gains?
Mere hair and scrubby bristles for his pains.
Now turn we to our friend who shears the Sheep:
Unlike the Pig, he lies as though asleep;
He wrestles not, he neither kicks nor shrieks,
In gentle tones the Shearer to him speaks,
And moves at will the shears o'er every part,
Nor fears a motion that his will may thwart.
To all men's eyes who watch the process here,
The labour's easy and the gain is clear:
Not scrubby bristles, but of finest wool
His lap not only, but his basket full,
Attest which Shearer hath the better gains,
Both as to profit and to gift of brains.
'Tis thus in life we not unfrequent see,
How some Men labour long and wearily,
T' achieve a purpose which they have in view,
Yet lose their labour and the object too;
The while that others easily attain
A kindred purpose, with completest gain.
In all men do, so much on tact depends,
That where that fails, success but rare attends;

That which is well confidered beft fucceeds ;
That which is well conducted fureft fpeeds :
Hence who in Shearing would no profit lack,
Should choofe a beaft with wool upon its back ;
Confider well all he would take in hand,
Nor mix with matters he don't underftand :
What one Man does, another fails to do ;
What's fit for me, may not be fit for you.

AL te wijs kan niet beginnen,
Al te geck kan niet verfinnen ;
Tusschen mal, en tusschen vroet,
Wint men wel het meefte goet.

Hy moet wagen
Die wil bejagen.

Die dit en gint geduerig schroomen,
Hoe konnen die tot rijckdom komen !

Gato guantato non prende mai forci.

'T Mach wayen, mil zijn, vloeyen, of ebben,
Die niet en waegt en mi niet hebben.

Sumptum faciat oportet is qui lucrum quærit.

Rien ne s'acquiert fans aventure, et rien fe conferve fans induftrie.

Chi guarda a ogni penna, non fa mai letto.

Sonder wagen niet vergaren,
Sonder wijsheyt niet bewaren.

Die elcke veer wil sien en raken,
Hoe kan die oyt een bedde maken !

Qui n'a guère,
N'a guerre.

Niemon en is geen erf.

Qui perd le sien, perd le sens.

M Y Light up to Heav'ns Manfions ftill doth move,
Seeking his native place of reft above;
But being ty'd in bondage to this frame,
It ftoopes to feeke his food, and feed his flame :
So ftill it finkes downeward, untill it turne
Into a fnuffe, and afhes ceafe to burne.

My mind, I know not how, longeth to flye,
Unto the Heavenly Courts and Saphire fky,
But ftill its plung'd, fo to the body bound,
That its compel'd to grovell on the ground :
Thus cralling for its food my foule can fret,
And tafting Lote, his Country doth forget.

FARLIE'S *Emblems.*

DRIVE THE NAIL THAT WILL GO.

Krepel wil altijds voor danfen.

CRIPPLE WILL ALWAYS LEAD THE DANCE.

ROSSING o'er a Village green,
Once I faw a pleafant fcene ;
Country lads and laffes gay,
Dancing on the firft of May,
Singing, fhouting, full of glee ;
'Twas a pleafant fight to fee
How they danc'd the May-pole round,
To the Bagpipe's merry found.

When the Piper ſhrilleſt play'd,
Greater was the noiſe they made;
And not one but ſeem'd to be
Almoſt mad with jollity.
But among them all was one
Who in noiſe the reſt outdone,
He, the leader of the game,
Was both bandy-legg'd and lame,
With a club-foot of ſuch ſize,
As quite fill'd me with ſurpriſe,
That ſo clumſy ſhaped a thing
Should be leader of the ring.
So it was ne'erleſs, and he
Firſt in everything would be:
Whatſoe'er was piped or ſung,
Cripple's voice the loudeſt rung.
Nimble though young Hans might be,
Great though Claes' agility,
And though Jordan knew the way
Smarteſt things to Tryn to ſay,
Whether jump, joke, ſing or bawl,
Cripple will eclipſe them all.

But, as on that Village green,
Juſt the ſame is elſewhere ſeen:
For in Town-life much the ſame,
Cripple oft will lead the game:
Though to limp is all he can,
Cripple is a clever man,
And whatever may befall,
Cripple muſt be firſt of all.
Is it not a curious thing,
When thereto our thoughts we bring,
That a ſhallow-pated fool
Juſt eſcaped from boarding ſchool,
Wanting mereſt common ſenſe,
Full of prate and vain pretence,

IS AS WELCOME AS SALT TO A SORE EYE.

Is the first to have his say,
And, unask'd, will lead the way
With opinions and conceits,
Where the world-wise hesitates?
    Would you know whence this derives!
'Tis that wisdom slower drives;
Wise men ever cautious weigh
That which they may have to say;
Give opinions ne'er by guess,
Nor unask'd their thoughts express;
But a Fool, all haste that he
Something may be thought to be,
Do or say, be what it may,
Will in all things lead the way.
Hence the saying doth derive,
" Fools are they who fastest drive,"
And its well known proverb twin,
" Cripple will the dance begin."

FATALIS imperitiæ pedissequa est Impudentia, et inanis jactatio.
  At Initium Sapientiæ, imperitiæ suæ agnitio.
Spes est melior de stulto, quàm de sapiente in oculis suis.—*Arab. Adag.*

  Qui plus balbutiunt, plus loquuntur.

  L'ABBATU veut toujours batter.

Godt bewaere my voor jemant die maer een boecksken geleten heeft.

Hoe slimmer timmer-man, hoe meerder spaenders.

  Veel roemen smelt een dummen grent:
  Een ydel vat homt aldermeest.
  Hoe slimmer wiel, hoe meer het raest.

Een penning in den spaer-pot maeckt meer geraes dans als hy vol is.

C'est la plus meschante roüe du chariot, qui mène le plus grand bruit.

In another sense.

  Quando la cornemusa è piena, comincia à sonare.
  When the bag-pipe's full it begins to sound.

Stultum, quàm semel stultum ferre, facilius est.—*Pub-Syrus.*

EVERY MOTHER THINKS HER OWN CHILD THE FAIREST.

AH wretch unworthy of thy infamous name,
    Burne not this sacred Church, to raise thy fame:
For though twas built by Heath'ns impiety,
Yet ought it not be thus deſtroy'd by thee:
Truſt me impiety every where is nought,
And Heath'ns their heathen profanenſſe dearly hought:
Let Toloſe gold, and Delphus robbery,
And Hammons ſandy ire this teſtifie:
It's thine, not my default, for I was made
For ſacrifice, and to make Creatures glad.
    Nothing ſo harmleſſe and ſo good can be,
    Which may not hurt, by mans impiety.

                      FARLIE's *Emblems.*

HE IS THE WISEST MAN

WHO DOES NOT THINK HIMSELF SO.

AMORES DOLORES Y DINEROS

NON PUEDEN ESTAR SECREDOS.

FIRE, COUGH, LOVE, AND MONEY, ARE NOT LONG
CONCEALED.

THIS Candle I would carry fo
   That neighbours cannot fee
A gleam of Light that may in aught
   Reveal a glimpfe of me;
For if I can, no one will watch
   Me then, and I may go

QUIS ENIM BENE CELET AMOREM?

Where'er I lift, without the fear
  That any one will know.
But still, in spite of all I do,
  I fear the light is seen;
Its rays still stream thro' all the holes
  And Lanthorn's chinks between;
Whatever care I take, howe'er
  I strive to shade it o'er,
Some gleams pierce thro' behind, or at
  The side, or thro' the door.
My neighbour's very old, and as
  Old people often are,
He's very much afflicted with
  A cough, and bad catarrhe;
But ne'ertheless, strange though it seem,
  As ev'ry one must own,
The good man has a great dislike
  To lie at night alone.
He's courting a young maiden now,
  And while he's so engaged,
He strives his best to stop the cough,—
  But 'twill not be assuag'd:
And while he sits and looks his best,
  To make his courtship sure,
The sprightly lass, tho' striving all
  She can to look demure,
Says, that is not the Music a
  Young Maiden's heart to gain,
And bids him rest content to sleep
  Alone, and not complain:
But if a Wife he's bent to have,
  The best thing he can do,
Is one of his own age to choose,
  Who has a bad cough too.
A fellow who to gain his bread,
  Runs errands here and there,
Found recently, a purse well fill'd
  With ducats, in the Square:

EN DE HANDT IS BY DE SMERTE.

With joy elate he took it home,
  And to his Wife he faid:
Look here! dear Trijn! I've found a prize!
  Our fortune now is made!
But you! you muft not breathe a word;
  So mind you what you do!
No one, Trijn, fave yourfelf, muft aught
  Of this good Wind-fall know!
No longer now with meffages
  Will I run here and there;
But like a Burgher live at eafe
  And have the beft of cheer!
Therefore ftitch thou this purfe infide
  Thy fleeve, or elfe fomewhere.
Trijn fwore fhe would, and with an oath
  To take the beft of care.
But, mark! e'en from that very time,
  The Wife began to fpend;
Drefs fine, prate large, and treat or this
  Or that dear-goffip-friend;
The Man, too, he will go no more
  With meffages—not he;
Such paltry jobs he fays are quite
  Beneath his dignity.
The Daughter, fhe is drefs'd as fine —
  The babe put out to nurfe,
'Tis wondrous ftrange! but money ne'er
  Will ftop within the purfe!
At length the truth gets wind, and lo!
  The man is prifoner made,
And mourns within a cell, that he
  Had left an honeft trade.
The fprightly Trijn in forrow blames
  Her foolifh fpendthrift-riot;
And all becaufe the money would
  Not reft in peace and quiet.

MY Light is gone, yet hope doth ſtill remaine,
That Light revived ſhall quick'n me againe.
I gaine by death, for ſo I longer laſt,
Life ſhall returne, after ſome houres are paſt.
All of us dye, when this our threed is ſpunne,
And cut, deaths drouſie ſleepe is then begunne.
After the ghueſt is gone, the Innes decay,
Our body's turn'd to rubbiſh and to clay;
Untill the ſoule returning doe poſſeſſe
Our bodies in Eternall happineſſe.

FARLIE's *Emblems.*

AVOR. E TOSSE, E ROGNA

CELAR NON TE BEBOGNA.

Elck Vogeltje singt soo't gebeckt is.

EVERY BIRD SINGS ACCORDING TO HIS BEAK.

T'IS an old Saying and a true,
　　That ev'ry bird fings its own note;
Nor can it any other do
　　But as permits its beak and throat,
Whene'er you rove thro' field or wood,
　　And well attend with ears and eyes,
You'll find the Proverb juft and good,
　　Whate'er the bird in fhape or fize.

EVERY MAN TO HIS TRADE.

Thofe which a hook'd fharp beak have got,
  Are for the moſt part Birds of Prey,
And bent alone on War, they wot
  No note of fong or minſtrelſy.
Whene'er near rivers, lake or flood,
  You chance a flat-beak'd bird to meet,
From groping in the fluſh and mud,
  Be fure his voice is never fweet.
The birds with longer flute-like beak,
  Might more be thought to fong inclin'd,
But in their thrumming note and fhriek,
  No turn for melody you'll find.
I therefore fay,—as far as fize
  And fhape of beak,—nor fear proteſt,
That of all birds beneath the ſkies,
  The little beaks they fing the beſt.
E'en thus among mankind, we fee,
  God gives the little now and then,
A talent rare and quality
  Which He gives not to bigger men.
Of little beaks, what bird like he
  Which night-thro' fings in wood and dale?
That feathered Soul of Harmony,
  That little beak, the Nightingale!
And would you feek a tuneful throat,
  You'll find throughout the feather'd throng,
The greater beak the harſher note,
  The fmaller beak the fweeter fong.
As with the Fowls of earth and air,
  Not fo with Man—he hath no beak,
But in his mouth beyond compare
  The nobler Godlike power to fpeak!
And when he fpeaks in fpirit kind,
  What note of bird more foftly fweet
To breathe the mufic of the mind,
  When kindred hearts and fpirits meet!
But when the mouth of Man outpours
  The blaſt of Paſſion's wrathful breath,

AND THE OX TO THE PLOUGH.

The Lion not more fiercely roars
  His angry note of blood and death!
Hence what befalls mankind between,
  Comes from a deeper fource exprefs'd,
Where fits, by ev'ry eye unfeen
  But God's, the impulfe of the breaft.
The Mouth commands, implores, decries,
  As moves the Heart, and gives thereto
The tone which moft its will implies,
  By force or foftnefs to fubdue.
Hence ye who fpeak in bitter tone,
  And fiercely wound another's heart,
Beware, and learn to curb thine own,
  Left it repay thee fmart for fmart.

As "by his ears the Afs is known,"
  A truth which no one can impeach,
"The Man," as Proverbs long have fhewn,
  "Is known as truly by his fpeech."

Die rede verrath das hertz.
  The speech betrays the man.

Au chant cognoît en l'oiseau,
Et au parler le bon cerveau.

Al suono si cognosce la midesza del vaso.

Was der Man kan,
Zeiget seine rede an.

Nanal nabala idaber.—*Turkish Adage.*

Id eft,
Stultus multa loquitur.

Out of the abundance of the heart the mouth speaketh.—*Matthew* xii. 34.

NATURE, propounds a dilemme, chufe I muſt,
    Either to dye by light, or rot by ruſt:
If I ſœke eaſe and reſt, then laſineſſe
Doth me confume with mouldy hoarineſſe;
But if I love to ſhine with glorious ray,
Then by my flames in teares I melt away.
Patience doth light'n this evill: I wiſh to live
In glorious light, and light to others give.

    This life is worne out with laborious toile,
    And ſlothfull reſt doth minde and body ſpoile;
    But yet it's better for to dye a ſparke,
    Than like a laizie moule to live in darke.

                  FARLIE's *Emblems*.

ALL ARE NOT HUNTERS THAT BLOW THE HORN.

ALL HEADS ARE NOT SENSE BOXES.

SILENCE SELDOM DOTH HARM.

SILENCE IS WISDOM, AND GETS FRIENDS.

HARES ARE NOT CAUGHT WITH BEAT OF DRUM, NOR BIRDS WITH TARTLETS.

HE who by beat of drum would catch a hare,
  Took the best means his purpose to defeat;
For soon as Puss the noise began to hear,
  With ears erect she quickly left her seat,

A MUCHA PAROLA OBRA POCA.

And making nimbly for the neareſt wood,
  Within its leafy cover got away,
Leaving our friend and dogs, however good,
  But little chance their fleetneſs to diſplay:
So that at eve, returning from his ſport,
  With empty game-bags and dejected look,
He found but little reaſon to report
  His ſtrange device—for not a hare he took!
He who in Council ſits, or would attain
  Knowledge of aught, or ſee his plans ſucceed,
Of all things firſt his tongue ſhould well reſtrain,
  Nor ſpeak a word beyond the matter's need:
For he who lets his tongue his wits outrun,
  And blabs his buſineſs into all men's ears,
Will find it ſpoil'd e'er yet it hath begun,
  And reap no other harveſt than their jeers.
In Love affairs as in State Government,
  The Lover and the Prince ſucceeds the beſt,
Who Silence keeps upon his mind's intent,
  Nor e'en permits his purpoſe to be gueſs'd.
Nothing by chatter ever yet was done,
  Conqueſt achiev'd, nor battle ever won;
But who with "ſtill tongue" doth his aim purſue,
  Wins beſt as Lover, and as Warrior too.

Πάλαι τὸ σιγᾶν φάρμακον βλάβης ἔχω.—ÆSCHYL. *Agam.*

Id eſt,

Silence pridem remedium damnis puto.

Eximia est Virtus, praestare silentia rebus:
  At contra gravis est culpa, tacenda loqui.—OVID. 2 *Art.*

Weise Leut' haben ihren Mund em Hetzen.
Alle'sogels schouwen d'openbare netten.

Chi dice tutto quel ch'egli sa, fa tutto quel ch'egli può, e mangia ciò ch'egli ha;
non gli resta niente.

Sag' nicht Alles das Du weist,
Glaub' nicht Alles das Du hörest,
Thue nicht Alles das Du kannst,
Wisse nicht Alles das Du lisest.

Multorum conscii pauca loquuntur.

In irā nihil decentius quàm cùm adest silentium.—PLUTARCH. *de Cohib. Ir.*

Vestigatoribus et venatoribus diurni nocturnique labores essent irriti, si non silentio priusquàm venabulis et impetu, feras interciperent.

CAROL. PASCHAL. *Virt. et Vit. cap. 32.*

Qui veut prendre oiseau, ne faut l'effaroucher.

Silence is the Sanctuary of Prudence.

A RESOLVE loudly expressed was never yet much esteemed. He who declares his intentions, exposes himself to censure, and if he does not succeed he is doubly unfortunate.

A man is always in time to speak, but not to refrain from speaking. We should speak as we make a Will; the fewer the words the less ground for law-suits. We should accustom ourselves thereto in matters of little moment, so that we may not fail to do so in affairs of importance. Whosoever is prompt to speak, is always upon the point of being conquered and convinced.

A heart without a secret is an open letter. Where there is depth, the secrets lie deep: for there must be great space, and a great vacuum, which will hold all that is thrown into it. Reserve derives from the great controul a man has over himself, and that is a real triumph. We pay tribute to all to whom we disclose our affairs. The security of Prudence consists in interior moderation. The things we would do should be kept to ourselves, and those which may be told may not be good to do.*

WE should hear and see, but thereby be silent.—GRACIAN'S *Maxims.*

S'IL y a beaucoup d'art a parler, il n'y en a pas moins a se taire.

LA ROCHEFOUCAULD.

THE carefull Matrone in her cell below,
  Let fall a groat, yet where fhe did not know:
Forthwith fhe tinnes a Light, then with her broome
She neatly fweepes the corners of the roome:
Thus from the duft and darkeneffe when fhe finds it,
More than the Phrygian Midas wealth fhe mindes it.
  Our foule a divine fparke fince that it fell
  Into Cimmerian darkeneffe of this cell,
  The foules true knowledge doth appeare no more
  Which goeth beyond Pygmalions richeft ftore.
  Then muft we light Cleanthes Lamp and find
  By ftudy, the loft treafure of our mind.

                              FARLIE's *Emblems.*

Culex fodit oculum Leonis.

LITTLE ENEMIES AND LITTLE WOUNDS

ARE NOT TO BE DESPISED.

THE GNAT STINGS THE EYES OF THE LION.

FRIENDS! come here and lift to me!
Something strange I would relate;
Should it prove of use to thee,
That will me well compensate.
Though so strong the Lion be,
Though so full of Majesty,

Though his eyes fo fiercely gleam
And fo terrible he feem;
That no man, whoe'er he be,
Can unmov'd his anger fee;
Yet the gnat, though he's fo fmall,
And fo flight of limb withal,
Is fo wond'rous brave and keen,
That the Lion oft is feen
Fill'd with dread as foon as he
Gnats perceives but two or three!
Yet the gnat doth not attack
Slyly, or behind his back;
But, firft, like a gen'rous foe,
Scorning all advantage low,
When the Lion comes in fight,
Sounds his challenge to the fight;
And forthwith bids him prepare
All his fierceft wrath to bear.
Nor doth he affault his foe
Where the leaft defence can fhow;
Though fo fmall, yet keenly bold,
Like a Paladin of old,
He the Lion fcorns t' affail,
On the flank or on the tail.
Front to front in open fight,
Heedlefs of the Lion's might,
Headlong at his face he flies,
And attacks his rage-lit eyes.
Where the Lion beft can fee
All his foe's boftility,
There the gnat, his rage defpite,
Rufhing 'mid their flafhing light,
Deeply ftings the fount of fight;
Till half blind and mad with pain,
The Lion flees acrofs the plain.

Let Arrogance by this be taught,
That whatfoe'er its Strength and Size,

There's nothing with more danger fraught
Than what is little, to defpife;
There's neither man nor brute fo great
But, like the Lion pictur'd here,
May learn to rue the wrath and hate
Of that which feem'd too fmall to fear.

INIMICUM quamvis humilem docti eſt metuere
A cane non magno ſæpè tenetur aper.—OVID. *Art.*

LEO etiam minimarum avium ſi pabulum.—CURTIUS.

UN petit homme abat bien grand' chesne.

EEN kleyn man, met een kleyn geweer,
Velt wel een grooten boom ter neer.

INEST et formicæ ſua bilis.
Habet et muſca ſplenem.

ET pueri naſum rhinocerotis habent.—MARTIAL, 1. *Ep.* 4

NE deſpicias debilem; nam Culex fodit oculum leonis.—STRADA.

A MOUSE in tyme maye bite in two a cable.—*Old Engliſh Proverb.*

TREAD a worm on the tayle, and it wil turne againe.—*Ibid.*

'Twas the mouse that ſet the Lion free.—*Ibid.*

WEN der feind iſt wie ein ameiſs,
So halt ihn doch für ein elephant.

UN petit moucheron pique bien un grand cheval.

EEN Kat ſiet wel op ein Koning.

A CAT maye looke at a Kinge.—*Old Engliſh Proverb.*

IL n'y a ſi grand, ni ſi ſage,
Qui de petit n'ait bien dommage.

IL eſt bien petit qui ne peut nuire.

GESELLEN, wilt uw wel beraden,
Hy is wel klein die niet kan ſchaden.

IL n'eſt pas ſage qui n'a peur d'un ſol.

ES iſt nicht an der groſſe gelegen,
Sonſt erlieff eine kuh einen haſen.

GRANDE Ville rien dedans;
Petite choſe nuiſt ſouvent.

ANCHE la muſcha ha la ſua collera.

DESPISE YOUR ENEMY, AND YOU

ONE candle difpels the darkeneffe of the night,
　　And many doe refemble Phœbus light:
One Sunne illight'ns the round globe every where,
What way th' horizon bounds the hemifphere:
If you ten thoufand thoufand Sunnes fhould fee
At once, O what a daylight would that be!

　　When Chrift amidft the clouds our doome fhall plead,
　　When Earth and Sea fhall render up their dead,
　　Saints more then ftarres at once fhall mount on hye,
　　As glorious Sunnes, to meete Chrift in the fkye.
　　That day fhall drive away the darkeneffe fo,
　　That after that, no day fhall darkeneffe know.

　　　　　　　　　　　　　　FARLIE's *Emblems.*

Amis sont comme le Melon; De dix souvent pas un de bon.

LIKE MELONS, FRIENDS ARE TO BE FOUND IN PLENTY,
OF WHICH NOT EVEN ONE IS GOOD IN TWENTY.

IN choofing Friends, it's requifite to ufe
The felf-fame care as when we Melons choofe:
No one in hafte a Melon ever buys,
Nor makes his choice till three or four he tries;
And oft indeed when purchafing this fruit,
Before the buyer can find one to fuit,

TRY THE ICE BEFORE YOU VENTURE ON IT.

247

He's e'en obliged t' examine half a score,
And p'rhaps not find one when his search is o'er.
Be cautious how you choose a friend;
For Friendships that are lightly made,
Have seldom any other end
Than grief to see one's trust betray'd!

BEPROEF uw vrient,
Beproef uw sweert,
Dat is uw groote schatten weert.

Who from mishap himself would guard,
Must prove his Friend as he'd prove his sword.

Les amis sont comme le melon,
Il faut essayer plusieurs, pour rencontrer un bon.

Le compagnon ou l'ami qui se tourne à inimitié, n'est-il pas une tristesse qui
demeure jusque à la mort!—*Syrach.* xxxvii. 3.

Esprouve tes amis selon ton pouvoir.—*Ibid.* ix. 11.

Si tu acquiers un ami, acquiers-le en l'esprouvant et, ne te fie point en luy
légèrement.—*Ibid.* vi. 7.

Κρίνει φίλους ὁ καιρός, ὡς χρυσὸν τὸ πῦρ.—MENANDER.

Id est,

Aurum probatur igne, amicus tempore.

As Fire, of Gold is e'er the surest test,
So Time doth prove the worth of Friendship best.

—

THERE is nothing better or more advantageous to mankind than prudent Diffidence;
'tis the guard and preservation of our lives and fortunes, our own security obliges us
to it; without it there would be no caution, without which no safety. . . . . For
who can secure himself of Man's heart, hid in the privatest corner of the breast,
whose secrets the tongue dissembles, the eyes and all the motions of the body
contradict!—ASTRY'S *Saavedra Faxardo.*

THE heart is deceitful above all things, and desperately wicked: Who can
know it!—*Jeremiah* xvii. 9.

(left margin) TRUST NO ONE TILL YOU HAVE EATEN A PECK OF SALT WITH HIM.

(right margin) CHOOSE A WIFE RATHER BY YOUR EAR THAN BY YOUR EYE.

False Judgment of the Many.

——— FORTUNE now
To my heart's hope!—gold, silver and base lead.
"Who chooseth me, must give and hazard all he hath."
You shall look fairer, ere I give or hazard.
What says the golden chest? ha! let me see:—
"Who chooseth me, shall gain what many men desire."
What many men desire!—That many may be meant
Of the fool multitude, that choose by Show,
Not learning more than the fond eye doth teach :
Which pries not to the interior, but, like the martlet,
Builds in the weather on the outward wall,
Even in the force and road of casualty.
I will not choose what many men desire,
Because I will not jump with common spirits,
And rank me with the barbarous multitudes.

SHAKESPEARE, *Merchant of Venice.*

BE not in haste to make new friends, nor to abandon those thou hast.—SOLON.

THE friendship of one wise man is better than that of a host of fools.—DEMOCRITUS.

CONTRACT no friendships with persons of less worth than yourself; you will derive more harm than benefit from them.—CONFUCIUS.

IF you desire to know a man's sentiments towards you, consult him upon something which interests you; his reply will reveal to you his whole heart, and whether he is your friend or your enemy.—PLATO.

TAKE not your friends at hazard; attach yourself only to men worthy of your friendship.—ISOCRATES.

THE friendship of the wicked has no duration; but Time worketh no change in the friendship of the good.—*Ibid.*

AMICUM ita habeas, posse ut fieri hunc inimicum scias.—LABERIUS.

BE on such terms with your friend as if you knew that he may one day become your enemy.

IT is better to untie, than to break a friendship.—CATO.

OUR friends sometimes exhibit vices which have long been concealed. The best thing then to be done is to abate your intercourse gradually. You should unstitch, but not tear.—CICERO.

IN secret silence of the night what's done
Is trust to me, concealed from the Sunne,
Phœbus did Mars and Venus' love betray,
And turning backe did greater crimes bewray:
What I doe see when witnesse is asleepe,
That like Harpocrates I closely keepe.

Let mortals learne to rule their tongue by me,
What lawfull secret they doe heare or see.

FARLIE's *Emblems.*

TRUST NO SECRETS TO A FRIEND, WHICH,

- IF REPORTED, WOULD BRING INFAMY. -

Ogni Gallo ruspà à se.

EVERY MAN WISHES THE WATER TO HIS AIN MILL.

EVERY MAN DOTH HIS OWN BUSINESS BEST.

EVERY COCK SCRATCHES TOWARDS HIMSELF.

GENTLE Reader, would you fee—
  Would you fomewhat wifh to know
Life, depicted truthfully,
And how things in this World go?
Simple though this Emblem be,
  In thefe bufy Fowls you'll find,
Symbolifed moft faithfully,
  Type moft true of Human Kind.

EVERY MAN FOR HIMSEL', QUO' THE MARTIN.

Well observe how ev'ry one,
  Picking, scratching here and there,
Looks to self, and self alone,
  Reckless how his neighbours fare.
Not a bird among them all
  Shews another bird a grain,
Tells him where he saw one fall,
  Nor assists, that he may gain:
Each, on his sole profit bent,
  Plies with beak and claws apace;
Woe to those who, negligent,
  Lose their chance, or miss the place!
Poultry of the self-same mould,
  Grasping, snatching all they can,
Have been found 'mong Young and Old,
  Ever since the World began.
Hence, young friends, if you would get
  Something in Life's Scramble too,
Keep a sharp look-out, nor let
  Others snatch the grain from you.

PROXIMUS sum egomet mihi.—TEMEST. *Aud.* iv. i

Wie brengt'er water tot sijn buer-mans huys, als sijn eygen huys brant?

Elk wil de boter op sijn koeck hebben.

Elck voor hem selven, en Godt voor ons allen.

Chacun tire l'eau à son moulin.
Chacun estudie pour soy.
Chacun tire à son profit.

Quisque sua case.
A la Cour du Roy
Chacun pour soy.

AIDE TOI, DIEU T'AIDERAS.

Es denckt ein yeder in seinen Sack.

Ogni grillo grilla à se.
Ognun tira l'acqua al suo mulino.

Tutti vogano alla galiota.
Tirano à se.

Ognuno carcia con la rete al suo fratello.

Les vertus se perdent dans l'intérêt comme les fleuves se perdent dans la mer.

Doet uto Saecken met Verstant.

A KING of England being at table in the house of one of his Courtiers, and finding the dwelling spacious and full of costly furniture and plate, although the owner had been in but very narrow circumstances previous to his appointment to the office he then held, the King became very desirous to learn from him how he amassed so much valuable property in so short a period; assuring him at the same time that no mischief should come to him if he told the truth. Whereupon the Courtier, thus pressed, said incontinently, that he had always been a man of exceeding diligence and industry: that he had constantly made it a rule to rise early in the morning, and always looked after his own concerns first; having completed which, he then attended to the King's business. Upon this the King made answer that he should have just done the very reverse; that he should have first minded the King's business, and then his own. The Courtier forthwith assured the King that he had thereby never done the least prejudice to his Majesty's affairs; for that he had only appropriated the time passed by others in sleep to the care of his own personal concerns; having effected which, he still got to the duties of his Office before those who, having indulged in long sleep, had got to theirs, and had neglected their own affairs.

Collige, non omni tempore messis erit.

Vergader graen in uwe schuren,
De Oegst en sal niet eeuwigh dueren.

Es ist alle tage Jagen-tag,
Aber nit alle tage fange-tag.

Provision faite en saison,
Fait de bien à la maison.

WHILST theeves doe digge at middle of the night,
        Working the works of darkenesse, not of Light;
No sooner through the window they me spy
But they affrighted turne their backes and fly.
This Light ill-doers no wayes can abide,
Simply revealing, what they falsely hide.

        There was a time when all in darkenesse lay,
        When mortals had a naturall night, no day ;
        Then Satan that arch-theefe did range abroad,
        Seeking in hearts and houses his aboad;
        But since that Chrifts bright Starre had shewne his Light,
        Great Pan is dead, the Devill is put to flight.

                                    FARLIE'S *Emblems.*

EVERY ONE THINKS HIS OWL, A FALCON.

EVERY MAN THINKS HIS OWN GEESE, SWANS.

Schoon voor-doen is half verkocht.

MANNERS MAKE A MAN, QUOTH WILLIAM OF WICKHAM.

MANNERS OFTEN MAKE FORTUNES.

WELL SET OFF IS HALF SOLD.

W HO would learn the art of wooing,
  And enfure the moft fuccefs:
Or acquire the art of doing
  Winning things with moft addrefs;
Need not learned volumes open,
  Writers old, in foreign fpeech,
But may fee it plainly fpoken
  In the leffon I now teach.

~ WELL BEGUN IS HALF DONE. ~

In your manner unpretentious,
  Yet, be diligent to shew,
Without being too sententious,
  All the pleasing things you know.

While you strive to please and serve all
  To attain the end in view,
Well examine, and observe all
  Without seeming so to do.
If in them you faults discover,
  Shew not you those faults perceive;
But if difficult to smother,
  That they're slight, let them believe.
By this rule abide in all things,
  And you'll be esteemed the more,
Nothing more success in life brings
  Than to hide your neighbour's sore.

Or in wooing, or when married,
  Bear this maxim still in mind:
Seldom Wedded Life miscarried
  Where both sides were somewhat blind.
Shew your brighter side to all men,
  And shew them that you see theirs,
Friends more readily you'll find then
  To advance your own affairs.
Who most taste and judgment uses
  To display his wares to view,
Best the Buyers eye seduces,
  And most quickly sells them too.

E^T quicunque potes dote placere, place.—Ovin.

——Occule mendas,
Quaque potes, vitium corporis abde tui.—*Idem*.

MULTA virum nescire decet. Pars maxima rerum
Offendit, si non interiora tegas.
Cui gravis oris odor, nunquam jejuna loquatur :
Et semper spacio distet ab ore viri.
Si niger, aut ingens, aut non sit inordine natus
Deus tibi, ridendo maxima damna feres.—OVID.

Ante omnia tamen.

PRIMA sit in nobis morum tutela, puellæ :
Ingenio facies conciliante placet.

DRENCT alles by, o frissche Jeughl,
Daer ghy uw lief door maken meugt.

METTRE en évidence et faire valoir les bonnes parties.

SCIPIO and other great men of antient and later times excelled in this useful art ; one which Ovid especially recommends to the attention of young persons as a fundamental rule of conduct.

C'EST la raison pourquoy les gens d'Estat conseillent aux Princes de monstrer leurs bonnes parties et de dissimuler leurs imperfections ; imitant le bon Architecte, qui loge (comme ils disent) ses plus beaux materiaux au frontispice de son bastiment.

JEAN MARNIX aux *Rers. Polit. Rel.* 5.

AENSIEN doet Vryen.
Het oogh is leydtsman van de min,
En vreught voor eerst de lusten in.
Wat het ooge niet en siet,
Dat begeert het herte niet.

Ex aspectu nascitur amor.

AEYTA un cepo
Parecera mancebo.

ACCOUSTRE un tronç, il semblera un jeune adolescent.
—OCULI sunt in amore duces.—PROPERT. 2. *El.* 12.

Ce qui plaist
Est à demy faict.

WAS das aug nicht sibt,
Beschwehrt das hertz nit.

Ἐκ τοῦ ὁρᾶφν γὰρ γίνεται ἀνθρώποις ἐρᾶν.

Id est,

Ex intuendo nascitur hominibus amor.
Ut vidi, ut perii !—VIRGIL.

AT lengthe my Store of Light hath reach'd its ende,
 Nor have I wherewithal more light to lende;
Greafe fpente, wick burned and fmoake all paffed away,
Of Light berefte, what bootes it here to ftay?
Yet while I am permitted to remaine,
It is to fhewe that I may ferve againe:
In patient Hope I therefore byde my time,
Until in me frefhe Light the Fates do trimme;
And if the greafe and wick be equale goode
To holde fuch Light, I reft of willinge moode.
For while to ferve, the means to us is given;
Who willinge ferve, fhall have their faults forgiven.

Geen Boom en valt ten eersten Slag.

ONE STROKE FELLS NOT AN OAK.

EH! friend, why then so sad, I pray?—
Thy woeful mien and looks betray
Some deep distress, some poignant grief,
To which I fain would bring relief.
Methinks some cross-grain'd, haughty maid
Hath thine affection ill repaid,

FAINT HEART NEVER WON FAIR LADY.

Treated thy suit with cold disdain,
And bade thee from all hope refrain?—
Yes, yes! Young man, I see -I know
'Tis that which thus dejects thee so;
But never be like this cast down!
Full many other men have known
A like repulse, when first they strove
To win a wav'ring woman's love.
Come, come! arouse thee from this mood;
It ill befits thee thus to brood,
And fret, and fume so woebegone
For loss of what may yet be won!
Cast but thine eye upon this tree,
And therefrom thou shalt quickly be
Instructed in the art to gain,
The fair one who hath caused thy pain.
This tree, which now so lowly lies,
But lately lifted to the skies
Its lofty crown; and though in size,
And girth, and grain so fair and sound,
Its pride is prostrate on the ground!
Thou seem'st to wonder how 'twas done;
How that alone the arm of one
So great a conquest could achieve?
List then to me, nor longer grieve:
For as that oak was fell'd, so thou
Thine haughty fair one's heart may'st bow.
Arm'd with an axe of trenchant steel,
I saw yon sturdy Woodman deal,
In long repeat, stroke after stroke
Against this massive heart of oak;
Till with the oft repeated blow
He brought the forest monarch low.

Learn thou from this, young man, no less,
　How truthful from all time was held
The pithy Maxim for Success:
　" At the first stroke no tree is fell'd."

ARE HA'F A GRAUT.

Would'ſt thou, my friend, as Lover ſo ſucceed,
  Do thou the like, nor one repulſe bemoan,
Succeſs, of Perſeverance is the meed ;
  " The conſtant drop will wear the hardeſt ſtone."

Non uno ictu dejicitur quercus.

Omnia conando docilis solertia vincit.

Mit viel Streichen wird der Stockfisch lind.

Veel slagen maken den Stock-vis murw.

Tὸ πολλὰ πλήγματα ἐκ πέτρα τρυπᾷ αἱ ἁμί.—Epici.

Dii sua labore dotes esse venales volunt.

Nul bien sans peine.

Omnia diligentiæ subjiciuntur.

Diligence passe Science.
  —Par est fortuna labori.

The wiſe and active conquer difficulties
By daring to attempt them : sloth and folly
Shiver and shrink at sight of toil and hazard,
And make th' impossibility they fear.—Rowe.

Perſeverance achieves Succeſs.

MANY are the ſayings of the Wiſe,
  In ancient and in modern books enroll'd,
Extolling Patience as the trueſt fortitude ;
And to the bearing well of all calamities,
All chances incident to Man's frail life,
Consolatories writ
With studied argument, and much perſuaſion fraught,
Lenient of grief and anxious thought ;
But with th' afflicted, in his pangs, their sound
Little prevails, or rather ſeems a tune
Harsh, and of diſſonant mood from his complaint :
Unleſs he feel within
Some source of conſolation from above,
Secret refreſhings, that repair his strength,
And fainting spirits uphold.—Milton.

MY CARE IS FOR THE FUTURE LIFE.

GOD ASSISTING, THERE IS NOTHING TO BE FEARED.

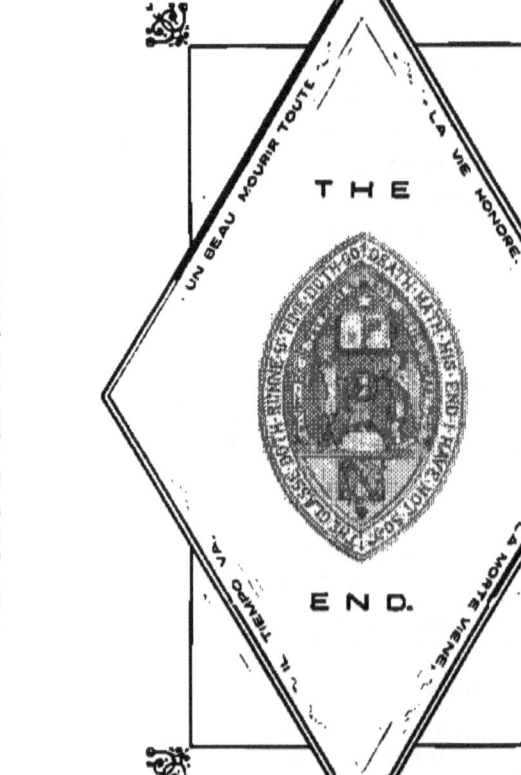

THE

END.

www.ingramcontent.com/pod-product-compliance
Lightning Source LLC
Chambersburg PA
CBHW031420020726
47499CB00005B/1524